Making a
Heart for God

Making a
Heart for God

A Week Inside a
Catholic Monastery

Dianne Aprile

Foreword by Brother Patrick Hart, OCSO

Walking Together, Finding the Way

SKYLIGHT PATHS PUBLISHING
WOODSTOCK, VERMONT

Making a Heart for God:
A Week Inside a Catholic Monastery

2002 First Quality Paperback Edition
© 2000 by Dianne Aprile

Photo credits: pages ii, 20, 22, 32, 42, 73, 91, 110, 152: Josh Shapero; pages 35, 71, 83, 97, 109, 149: Brother Paul Quenon.

Library of Congress Cataloging-in-Publication Data
   Aprile, Dianne.
   Making a heart for God : a week inside a Catholic monastery / Dianne
      Aprile ; foreword by Patrick Hart.
         p.   cm. — (A week inside)
   Includes bibliographical references and index.
   ISBN 1-893361-14-4 (hardcover)
   1. Abbey of Our Lady of Gethsemani (Trappist, Ky.) 2. Monastic and religious life. I. Title. II. Series.
BX2525. T733 A67 2000
255'. 125—dc21   00-011792

ISBN 1-893361-49-7 (paperback)

10 9 8 7 6 5 4 3 2 1

Manufactured in the United States of America

SkyLight Paths, "Walking Together, Finding the Way" and colophon are trademarks of LongHill Partners, Inc., registered in the U.S. Patent and Trademark Office.

Walking Together, Finding the Way
Published by SkyLight Paths Publishing
A Division of LongHill Partners, Inc.
Sunset Farm Offices, Route 4, P.O. Box 237
Woodstock, VT 05091
Tel: (802) 457-4000   Fax: (802) 457-4004
www.skylightpaths.com

For her role in setting me on the path to Gethsemani,
this book is dedicated to my aunt, Aileen Elizabeth
Bauman, whose prayers and love know no end.

Other books in the
A Week Inside Series

Contents

Foreword

In *Basic Principles of Monastic Spirituality*, one of his early writings, Thomas Merton expressed the essence of the monastic charism in a striking way. "In the night of our technological barbarism, monks must be as trees which exist silently in the dark and by their vital presence purify the air." As he did in all his writings, Merton saw the vocation of the monk as a witness to the reality of God's love, a radical response to the Gospel, and as one where being takes precedence over doing. The work in which the monk is engaged is infinitely less important than who he is as a person, a disciple of the Lord. One is reminded of the early desert tradition in Egypt where the monks advocated weaving baskets as a discipline: baskets woven one day by the monks were undone the following day. Today, in our consumer society, we might adjust that image and allow baskets to be sold at the local market or on the Internet.

Dianne Aprile understands this well as she knows the monastic life from the inside. Some years ago she wrote an engaging article on the Abbey of Gethsemani for the *Louisville Courier-Journal*. The monks were deeply impressed by this perceptive essay, and on the strength of it commissioned her to write a volume commemorating the 150th anniversary of Gethsemani's existence. She had not only visited Gethsemani's archives many times and interviewed a good cross-section of the monks, but also traveled to the mother house of Melleray in France, as well as several of the foundations made by Gethsemani in the United States, such as the Monastery of the Holy Spirit, near Atlanta, Georgia, and Holy Trinity Abbey in Utah. The result of her research was the handsome, illustrated book, *The Abbey of Gethsemani: Place of Peace and Paradox*, which was deservedly well received.

In preparing the present volume, Dianne was able to interview the last three Gethsemani abbots as well as many of its guestmasters of the past dozen years. What is especially remarkable about this book is that she was able to speak at length with so many of the ordinary monks, like the brother with the green thumb who tended the flowers, or the lay brother who spent most of his monastic life making cheese and who loved every minute of it. These monks were able to provide the author with an authentic day-to-day experience of the monastic life as seen by those who lived it fully. She soon found a common denominator regarding the attraction of the monastic life for so many in the community: God spoke to their hearts, and they answered the call. Although there were similar aspirations, each monk interviewed revealed his own unique story, his personal response to the Lord.

What *Making a Heart for God* does so compellingly is to explain the motivations that brought these men to the monastery and the problems involved for each in trying to be faithful to such a vocation for a lifetime. Likewise, the author's ability to enter into the journeys of those who were making retreats adds a special dimension to the book. The presence of guests and retreatants is a real source of encouragement for the monks, who see these men and women—young and old, and of various religious persuasions, who have heavy responsibilities in the world, yet who take time from their busy schedules—allowing themselves to be drawn into the desert place to be alone with the Lord for a few days or a week or longer. The monks understand this, and become more conscious of their own special vocations to live their entire lives for the sake of the Lord and to love their brothers and sisters in the world.

Dianne Aprile makes the connection between the monks who live in the monastery and those who come for a time of rest and retreat: all are in search of the "one thing necessary." *Making a Heart for God* is first of all the work of God in the lives of those who respond with ready hearts to this amazing and powerful grace. What follows demonstrates how well the author has identified with the inner search in what in the monastic tradition is called "The School of Charity." May the Lord continue to inspire many persons to respond to this ongoing invitation as we enter the new millennium.

Brother Patrick Hart, ocso
Abbey of Gethsemani

Acknowledgments

For their candor, their enthusiasm, and their boundless generosity in sharing their stories with me over the years, I wish to thank the monks of the Abbey of Gethsemani. They have always made me feel a welcome guest in their home. I am deeply grateful to Father Timothy Kelly and Father Damien Thompson, past and present abbots of Gethsemani, for giving me permission to explore, openly and unfettered, the daily life of their Trappist house, and to use throughout this book material derived from my interviews and research there.

To Brother Patrick Hart I extend my thanks for bringing his peerless perspective to the foreword of this book. For helping me to select and kindly permitting me to reproduce their photographs of Gethsemani, I am indebted to Josh Shapero and Brother Paul Quenon.

For assistance along the way, I also thank Anne McCormick of the Merton Legacy Trust; Michael Brown of Cistercian Lay Contemplatives; Vanessa Hurst of the Benedictine Association of Retreat Centers; and the many family members and friends of the monks of Gethsemani, whose stories helped round out the picture of life there.

Most especially, I wish to acknowledge Brother Joshua Brands and Brother Raphael Prendergast for their invaluable assistance, exceptional kindness, and divinelike patience throughout this project. Two better guides to the inner workings of a modern monastery could not be found—nor could two dearer friends.

I am grateful for the vision and tenacity of all those with whom I had the pleasure of working at SkyLight Paths Publishing. My special thanks go to David O'Neal for his creative and wise counsel as editor of this book.

Finally, to my husband, Ken, and our son, Josh: Thank you both for all the ways, large and small, that you made it possible for me to write this book. Your love inspires me.

Making a
Heart for God

Step by Step: The Journey Begins

The essential thing is . . . to climb step by step to the perfection of charity and to strive to be of one will with God. —THE SPIRITUAL DIRECTORY OF THE REFORMED CISTERCIANS

Hearing the Call

You see it first through the cedar and sycamore as you wind your way south along Highway 247, a gray ribbon of state road that weaves together the wooded hills and green meadows of this secluded stretch of central Kentucky. First you catch a glimpse of church steeple, then a flash of wall running alongside the road, and maybe, if you don't blink, a glimmer of white crosses on a grassy slope.

You turn slowly into the tree-lined driveway at an intersection marked by a flashing red light. There, beneath a canopy of sweet gum trees, you find yourself face to face with the oldest Trappist monastery in America, struggling with the contradictions it immediately poses.

It looks, at once, medieval and modern. It looms before you like a castle, yet is also stark and spare. It feels isolated despite a parking lot packed with cars. It beguiles the imagination, drawing you closer, even

3

as it intimidates and unsettles you. It is clearly as contemplative as contemporary life gets. Yet, it takes no time at all to discover that this is a place where not just the spirit moves, but the body and mind as well.

Welcome to life inside a twenty-first-century Catholic monastery. The Abbey of Gethsemani, in the heart of Kentucky's bourbon country, is arguably the best-known Catholic abbey in the world today, due primarily to the celebrity of its most famous monk, the late Thomas Merton. It was founded in 1848 by a pioneering tribe of French Trappists (or Cistercians of the Strict Observance, as Trappists are formally known), and it carved a special niche for itself in the post-World War II years after Merton's autobiography—*The Seven Storey Mountain*—became a surprise best-seller. Known as Father Louis to his brothers at Gethsemani, Merton went on to publish another forty books and hundreds of essays and articles on subjects ranging from Sufism and civil rights to literature and Vietnam-era politics.

But for all its celebrity, the Abbey of Gethsemani is essentially like any other monastery anywhere in the world—a paradoxical place. To the outside observer just settling in for a week of retreat, it can seem a house of contradictions. The monks rise at 3:00 AM each day, as Cistercian monks have done for nearly one thousand years. Rather than tending crops and livestock as their forebears did, however, today they support themselves at computer keyboards and Internet websites, promoting and selling their homemade food products.

No question, the paradox of modern monasticism (both its male and female versions) is part of the huge appeal it has today to visitors of all faith traditions, young and old, urban and suburban, serious seekers and the just-plain-curious. Who, after all, wouldn't be intrigued by the particulars of this ancient form of communal living, dedicated (the Internet notwithstanding) to prayer, mindful work, sacred reading, patient reflection, and the surrender of one's ego in contemplation? Who wouldn't be struck by its stark contrast to the nonstop information gathering and sound-bite analyses of the broader culture? Who wouldn't wish, in some fashion, for a comparable balance in life?

Granted, there has been a sharp decline over the past three decades in what Catholics call "monastic vocations"—a term used to describe the men and women who are called to religious communities like the one at Gethsemani. For more than fifteen centuries, since the day the first Egyptian hermit headed for the desert, members of that small but enduring minority have chosen to dedicate their lives to seeking God in the relative isolation of a monastery. Today the monastic life continues to attract potential monks and nuns (as the former's female counterparts are known). Yet the number of those who make the actual commitment has slipped considerably since the late 1960s.

Making a retreat on the grounds of a Catholic men's or women's monastery, on the other hand, is an increasingly popular spiritual endeavor for Americans today. At Gethsemani, where a guesthouse renovation in the 1980s opened the door to female retreatants for the first time, the number of overnight visitors has increased dramatically over the past decade. At present, it's not at all unusual for retreat rooms to be booked twelve months in advance. Some retreatants sign up routinely for a particular week or month, spending special anniversaries or seasons in the same retreat rooms year upon year.

Individuals make retreats for all sorts of reasons. It's no secret that American culture can be overwhelming and exhausting. Many of us sign up for rooms in a retreat house to escape from the chaotic rhythms of modern life, the way some people take to the mountains or a beach. We arrive hungry for a little peace and quiet, a generic spiritual getaway. Others of us come to pray and meditate on specific concerns, to reflect on the path our lives have taken, to discern what choices will face us down the road. Some of us seek a monk's guidance during a retreat. Others want the space and freedom to go it alone. Gethsemani, like most Trappist monasteries, offers both options.

Unquestionably, part of the appeal of the monastic retreat comes from a desire to observe at close range, and if possible to enter into, the uncommon daily rituals of monks. Intuitively, we recognize that the life of a monk is countercultural, that it goes against the grain of our own path; and that makes us wonder what draws men to it, why it's been a viable lifestyle since the third century.

The monk isn't like your next-door neighbor or your cubicle mate at the office. He is not likely to pack a pager or a palmtop. Even his small bedroom, called a "cell," has no phone on the nightstand, no TV (cable or otherwise), no alarm clock tuned to an all-news station. It is safe to assume that he has not experienced road rage lately; in fact, he may not have driven a car for years. He does not day-trade on the Internet. He does not carry a credit card. He does not bank at ATMs. How could he? He has no money.

So what *does* he do? What keeps him occupied? What is it that brought him to this quiet, out-of-the-way place so peacefully out of sync with the pace of mainstream Western culture? And what is it that keeps him there, day after day, year after year, until a lifetime has come and gone?

Why is it that we, in turn, are drawn to learn more about the monastic life? Is it the lure of a disciplined lifestyle? The commitment to spiritual quest? The ancient rituals, the reflective rhythms, the religious tradition? Is it the lure of a life that's simpler, more basic, less materialistic, more closely connected to the cycles of nature? Is it the answer to a distinctly heard call from God, a leap of great faith? Or is it an escape, a cop-out, a last resort?

These are the questions that draw us, skeptics as well as true believers, to the retreat houses and public gardens of monasteries like Gethsemani. It is what we are wondering as we watch the monks go about their business, chanting psalms in the abbey church before dawn, or digging weeds on their knees in a sunny garden, or assigning guest rooms from behind a lobby desk.

For all their charm, these activities, even when carried out in church, reveal only the public face of a monastery. They are behaviors that any accidental passerby may observe. Encounters between monk and visitor on the public side of the cloister wall provide a superficial glimpse, at best, of monastic life and offer the merest hint of why it has endured, in one form or another, for nearly two millennia. Like the first-time visitor's initial sighting of the abbey through the trees along the highway, an outsider's view of monastic life reveals a hint of the whole picture— but only a hint. And those hints are what stir up in us a desire to make a longer visit.

Inside the Cloister Gate

In the mid-1990s, when I was writing the history of the Abbey of Gethsemani, then-abbot Father Timothy Kelly gave me a set of keys to the abbey archives. As a journalist living in Louisville, just an hour's drive from Gethsemani, I had written frequently about the place and, consequently, earned the trust of the abbot. "Come and go as you need to," Father Timothy told me. That meant crossing from the public to the private side of the cloister wall to the abbey archives, a suite of rooms on the top floor of a three-story red-brick building.

I accepted this privilege with more than a little humility. Few individuals have been granted such access to the "other side of the wall," where the true monastic life is lived out, hour by hour. Women, in particular, have been rare visitors to the cloistered areas of men's monasteries, Gethsemani included. As recently as my own youth in the 1960s, females were prohibited from entering the monastic "enclosure," as it is called. For Catholic women at that time, an unauthorized step across that threshold carried the automatic penalty of excommunication from the church. Suffice it to say, the gift of my own ring of keys to the archives was not only a researcher's dream come true, but also a sign of the sea change in monastic life that occurred in the latter half of the twentieth century.

While researching the abbey's 150-year history, I also had the chance to get to know, up close and personally, many of the monks who live there. Some of those I interviewed were long-timers, men who arrived in the post-World War II heyday of the monastery, when new recruits were so plentiful that a makeshift dormitory had to be thrown together in the courtyard to house them all. Others were relative newcomers, men who heard the call later in life and left careers as teachers and businessmen to enter Gethsemani. From the inside of the enclosure, I was privy to a perspective on the monks different from that which the typical visitor or retreatant gets.

And it is this perspective that I share with you in the following chapters. The focus is on the daily routines of the Catholic monk, the fabric of his richly textured spiritual life: the prayers, public and private; the sacred reading, mealtime rituals, and workday obligations; the caretaking of the community's elders, and the relationships among brothers. You will experience all this in the intimate, hour-by-hour way that a retreatant would experience it during a week's stay at Gethsemani. You will also get a glimpse of the day-to-day spiritual and organizational challenges faced by the monks of Gethsemani.

Trappists like to say that the life of a monastery, organizationally complex yet soul-simple, exists as a sign of God's love in the world. During the course of my research I was reminded again and again of how that sign is constantly being broadened and deepened. One such reminder came in the summer of 1996, when Gethsemani hosted a long-anticipated international conference of Eastern and Western monks. Zen, Theravadin, Tibetan, and other Buddhists from Sri Lanka, Cambodia, Thailand, and across the United States came together with nuns and priests and lay brothers from Catholic monasteries around the world. His Holiness the Dalai Lama, the exiled spiritual leader of

Tibet, was the guest of honor at that 1996 conference, which was an outgrowth of a series of one-on-one meetings the Dalai Lama had with Merton in 1968, just before the Trappist died. The 1996 meeting was not the Tibetan monk's first visit to Gethsemani; most likely it will not be his last. And that is as it should be, in the best monastic tradition of hospitality and spiritual dialogue. If a monastery like Gethsemani is to be a true sign of God's work in the world, then it follows that the monks who inhabit it must engage in conversation with the world's great spiritual traditions—Buddhist, Jewish, Muslim, Hindu, and the like.

Once again, then, the paradox arises: In the process of striving for union with God through solitude, silence, and Christian faith, the Catholic monk reaches out to the world in all its diversity and extends an embrace of peace.

Seeking the Presence of God

Monks have a tradition of storytelling. It is the way they pass on to the next generation the lessons they have learned. In that spirit, I share a story of my own, an experience from one of my first visits to Gethsemani.

The story begins on a rain-swept path near the edge of a woods, early in the morning. Setting out for a brisk walk before breakfast, I am by myself, moving along a quiet trail, catching some time away from the crowd staying in the retreat house. I keep my head down, watching my step, until I feel a sudden urge to look up. To my surprise, I see five lithe-limbed deer standing, still as statues, ten feet or so from my own startled heart.

One of the five, a lovely, graceful deer, catches my gaze. We stand there, eyes locked, for what seems like forever but in truth lasts only a few unforgettable minutes. The deer eventually bolts, with his friends following him across a creek and up a ridge, their white tails streaking like ghosts through the glistening trees.

For years, the image of the deer has stuck with me. I have turned the story over and over in my mind. I have written it in a poem, described it in an essay, repeated it in conversations.

Ultimately, I recognized it as a metaphor for life inside a monastery. The locked-eye gaze represents the ideal of silent union with God that is the crux of all monastic practice. The rain-swept trail suggests the spiritual journey of the monk—one that leads him away from the crowd, down a quiet path, to the presence of God alone.

In essence, my encounter with the deer underscores the trio of monastic principles—seclusion, silence, and solitude—that shapes each day for Cistercian monks and sustains them in their quest for communion with God. The encounter made me want to see the deer again, to search them out on every path, just as the monk hunts the divine presence in all things at all times.

This book is a look behind the scenes of what you might observe during a one-week retreat in a Catholic monastery—the day-to-day life of the Catholic monk. As we begin our observations, it's important to keep in mind that while we will be observing monks at a men's monastery, most of what we see applies also to nuns living in a women's monastery. Also bear in mind that the daily routines of monastic life vary from monastery to monastery, depending on many factors, including whether the community is Benedictine or Cistercian, male or female, large or small.

One other note: In general, the words *abbey* and *monastery* will be used synonymously throughout this book. A monastery, in Catholic terminology, is the dwelling place of monks, nuns, or other religious who are living a communal life under a common rule. Strictly speaking, however, an abbey has a more specific meaning among Trappists and Benedictines. For Trappists, it signifies an autonomous monastery of monks or nuns, governed by an abbot or abbess, living according to the Rule of St. Benedict. Some monasteries today are not abbeys but priories, headed by priors, while some others follow a rule other than the one written by St. Benedict, who founded the first abbey at Monte Cassino near Rome in the sixth century. In the final analysis, all abbeys are monasteries, but not all monasteries are abbeys.

1

An Out-of-the-Way Place: Respite from a Harried World

Come by yourselves to an out-of-the-way place
and rest a while.   —MARK 6:31

Getting There

It is early on a Monday morning, the first workday of the monastic week, the day most guests arrive at Gethsemani to begin their retreats. As the monks go about their usual chores and prayers, I leave my home, fifty miles north of the monastery, to join them for a week-long retreat.

About twenty minutes into the drive, as always, I feel a change come over me. It is equal parts anticipation and relief. I feel I am shedding a skin: the crust of frantic, fragmented, postmodern life. I'm letting go of the hard layers of stress and noise, commotion and conflict, beepers and buzzers, vibrating pagers. I can almost taste fresh air on my lips. The memory of it lingers from my last retreat at the abbey.

There is an interstate highway sign about fifteen miles outside of Louisville, my home, alerting drivers to the exit to Brooks Road. What I notice, invariably, is a shift in my physical attitude as I pass that visual landmark. My shoulders relax. My hands grip the steering wheel with a little less pressure. I breathe more slowly, more deeply. And I feel a gentle smile, spreading from my eyes down to my mouth, taking over the territory that was previously occupied by my cool, noncommittal urban gaze. I think of the contemporary Buddhist teacher Thich Nhat Hanh, who advocates wearing a "half-smile" as our greeting to the world upon waking in the morning. "A smile," he has written, "confirms you are in complete mindfulness."

Over the past decade I have made my way countless times along the tree-lined avenues that traditionally serve as entryways to Cistercian monasteries. Through Georgia pines, up a curving canyon road from Salt Lake City, past the Breton villages and farmlands of western France—each time I have felt the same promise of respite, same stirring of hope, same surrendering of my protective mask.

Certainly there is a feeling of entering sacred space at these times. It is as if the land were somehow consecrated by the people who preceded me—by their presence and their prayers and their perseverance. At Gethsemani, the spiritual history of the rolling fields and wooded knobs of this part of central Kentucky has been mythologized by generations of visitors and neighbors as a regional "Holy Land." The area's reputation as sacred ground is well earned; historical facts support it. Before the arrival in 1848 of the forty-four Trappists from Melleray, France, who founded the abbey, an earlier band of French Trappists had briefly settled on a site in Kentucky not far from where Gethsemani now sits. Two pioneer communities of Catholic women—the Sisters of Charity of Nazareth and the Sisters of Loretto at the Foot of the Cross—also had their beginnings nearby, decades before Gethsemani was founded.

In fact, the Sisters of Loretto sold to the Trappists the land they now inhabit. The sisters, who now live in neighboring Marion County, are also responsible for the monastery's name today. Gethsemani—the garden in which Christ prayed before his betrayal and arrest—was what they called one of the buildings on their property. The monks retained the title when they took possession of the land, calling their new home the Abbey of Our Lady of Gethsemani, in the Trappist tradition of devotion to Mary, the mother of Jesus.

The land is also rich with the memory of other highly spiritual communities of men and women. Not far from the monastery, buildings still stand that once housed a settlement of Shakers, known as Pleasant Hill. In keeping with the spirit of monastic life, those celibate Protestants left as their musical legacy a lilting folk song, "Simple Gifts." Prior to the Shakers, several tribes of Native Americans also occupied nearby land. Like the Trappists today, these early communities respected and appreciated the power of silence, solitude, and simplicity, and preferred, for the most part, to live, work, and worship in contemplative, communal ways.

Letting Go

We all need a center to which to return . . . some sort of hope, some harbor, some retreat. —FATHER MATTHEW KELTY, MONK OF GETHSEMANI

Visitors to Cistercian and Benedictine monasteries often speak of feeling drawn to a haven, a safe place, a refuge that the frenzied world cannot penetrate. I have felt it time and again, usually as early in my journey as the Brooks Road highway sign and always by the time I reach Gethsemani's tree-lined entrance, which the monks refer to as "the avenue." There is a majesty to this long, straight, blacktop boulevard lined with towering sweet gums planted nearly a century ago to replace the original elms brought over as saplings from France.

The sensation of leaving things behind—answering machines, the Dow and NASDAQ, the carpool schedule—is a very real one, an autonomic response to distancing oneself from the clamor and tumult of contemporary American life. But some would say this sensation of surrender is not so different from that experienced by the so-called

Desert Fathers, the hermits of early Christianity. St. Anthony, the father of Christian monasticism, was the first of these "protomonks" to live alone in the Egyptian desert. In the year 285 he literally left behind everything he owned and headed out for the wilderness in a grand gesture that spoke both to the vow of poverty later sworn by the monks who would follow him and to the symbolism of abandoning oneself to a pure dependence upon God's love as the answer to all spiritual and physical needs.

Any entry into the monastic world—either then or now, as visitor or as monk—involves an invitation to the "desert"; that is, to the surrender of all to God. This can be a disconcerting proposal, as is evident from the candid writings of later Christian mystics like St. John of the Cross, who popularized the phrase "dark night of the soul." In much the same way that Anthony and his disciples must have felt when they left their comfortable peasant lifestyles to seek God in the extreme setting of the desert, the modern retreatant often finds the first flash of Trappist discipline and architecture more than a bit forbidding—a path and a place as austere as they can be hospitable.

Monasticism, Christian or otherwise, is a response to the human urge to take time out from the hectic tempo of the world to consider the true meaning of life. The monk trusts that in the process of leaving behind the material world, he will find the meaning of existence in union with God.

In his book *The Wisdom of the Desert*, Merton speaks of the early desert hermits as men and women who had not "the slightest identification with the superficial, transient, self-constructed self." Today, whoever accepts Gethsemani's invitation to "come and rest a while" is likely to leave with a more explicit understanding of Merton's point in that passage. He was describing an ancient, existential quest as well as a fundamentally Christian one: the search for the "authentic" self, stripped of the illusions of temporal reality.

No question about it, a week spent at a Catholic monastery, undistracted by the blare of twenty-first century culture and technology, is almost guaranteed to provoke a bout of serious meditation on the "self-constructed self." It's not surprising that the calling of many a monk crystallized during a week spent on retreat at a monastery.

Getting Around

A brother came and stayed with a certain solitary, and when he was leaving, he said: "Forgive me Father, for I have broken in upon your Rule." But the hermit replied, saying: "My Rule is to receive you with hospitality and let you go in peace."

—THOMAS MERTON, *THE WISDOM OF THE DESERT*

Gethsemani rests in the heartland of Kentucky, close to the geographical center of the commonwealth. It is a landscape of peaks and valleys, similar to the French countryside so familiar to the monks who founded the monastery in the decade before the start of the Civil War. It must have been a comfort to them: the isolated acreage, set amid the rolling fields and gently tapered hills known as knobs. It remains a comfort today to the descendants of those French founders.

"When you have a bunch of men living together in community, I think we have a tendency to have a lot of sharp edges and rough spots and moments when we need something to gentle us and to calm us," a Gethsemani novice, or monk-in-training, once told me. "And what better to calm us than the hills and the knobs, as God made them? We can go out to the woods and relax and let our guards down—just sit on the porch, so to speak—and watch."

Rustic settings suit the manual-labor component of a monk's life, too. As followers of the Rule of St. Benedict, the monks of Gethsemani and all the Cistercians who preceded them have traditionally been farmers who worked the land and raised livestock to support themselves. As such, they tended to build their monasteries in remote, rural areas. Cistercians are among the thousands of Benedictine monks and nuns today who still follow the Rule, which was written in the sixth century by the Italian monk Benedict of Nursia. Benedict placed high value on a balanced life of work, prayer, and sacred reading. Isolated farming country, like that surrounding Gethsemani, was believed to be the most nurturing atmosphere for both the physical lifestyle and the spiritual pulse of the Christian monk.

What the first-time visitor to Gethsemani sees, approaching the abbey, are thousands of acres of woods, meadows, hiking trails, wild-flower fields, lakes, ponds, timber land, gardens, and farm plots spreading in all directions on both sides of the road. To the initial 1,500 acres that the Trappists bought from the Sisters of Loretto, nearly a thousand more have been added over the past 150 years.

It is an idyllic setting that one approaches, both in terms of land-scape and architecture. "We live in rural Kentucky, and though it is not rich farming country, it is not at all hard to look at," Father Matthew Kelty, a long-time monk and author of Gethsemani, has written. "It is not lush, but in early summer it is not far from it. . . . A blue haze gives a mystic quality to the whole landscape which even the roar of an occasional passing jet high overhead . . . or a passing semi-trailer from a Seagram distillery nearby cannot wholly dispel."

The abbey's last major renovation stripped away the neo-Gothic trappings of the church and other monastic buildings. The nineteenth-century founders of Gethsemani had attempted to duplicate, with faux vaulting and plaster saints, the Old World glory of medieval Benedictine architecture. But early Trappist churches, including the one at Gethsemani's twelfth-century mother house in France, tended to be spare and simple. The massive renovations at Gethsemani in the 1960s and the later remodeling of the guesthouse have striven to restore that original Cistercian clarity of line and form. Ornate arches and dark European glass were ripped out of the church, and the walls and ceilings stripped back to their essential composition of brick and wood beam.

On my first visit to Gethsemani, in 1990, Brother Luke Armour, who was guestmaster at the time, described the renovation process with a sentence that still comes to my mind whenever I visit. The sentence applies not only to the stripping away of wood veneers, but also to the monk's approach to his own spiritual life: "Remove the bogus; reveal the authentic."

The old gatehouse that served as a transition point between the world and the monastery for more than a century was also taken down. The most obvious point of entry today is the massive doorway to the church. It is reached by a long, sweeping walkway that leads first to a broad set of rising stairs and then to a spacious porch. If the intended effect of this extended approach to the church is to heighten one's sense of anticipation and mystery, it is certainly successful. I have made my way up that stairway many times on the eve of Easter, as part of the hundreds of Kentuckians in the candlelit crowd who join the monks each year for the dramatic outdoor service that precedes Gethsemani's midnight Mass. I have also walked along it at dawn on my way to join the monks in morning prayers. No matter the time of day, it never fails to stir in me a feeling of gratitude for the presence of such a place and for the chance to tap into the life that goes on there.

Before reaching the church, however, two other portals punctuate the walkway, each opening to a different public view of monastic life. To the left, inside a small alcove, a doorway opens into the retreat house lobby. Carved above the door is the word PAX ("peace"), flanked by the numbers 1098 and 1848, the founding dates, respectively, of the Cistercian order at Citeaux, France, and the Abbey of Gethsemani at Trappist, Kentucky. This lobby is where arriving retreatants check in with the monk on desk duty and visitors can spend a restful hour or two

Interior of a retreat room. Retreat house rooms are simply furnished, usually with desks and comfortable chairs for reading.

sitting in the meditation garden, reading or silently praying. Adjacent to the garden is a small plot of identical white crosses, a supplemental cemetery marking the graves of a few dozen monks.

Directly across from the doorway to the retreat house, on the right side of the walkway, a plain iron gate provides an opening in an otherwise solid wall. Through the gate rails is a view that takes in a winding path, a pond with lily pads, and the doorway to the south wing of the monastery. The gate is an entrance to the monastic enclosure, where only monks—and invited visitors—are allowed. Above this gate are two words: GOD ALONE.

Renovated in 1989, the retreat house is among the busier ones in the Cistercian Order. It has private rooms for thirty-one guests. Prior to the renovation, only men were permitted to stay overnight. But Father Timothy Kelly, then abbot, encouraged his community to attach private

SKYLIGHT PATHS PUBLISHING
SUNSET FARM OFFICES RTE 4
PO BOX 237
WOODSTOCK VT 05091-0237

Place
Stamp
Here

We hope you will enjoy this book and that you will find it useful and use it to enrich your life.

Book title: _____

Your comments: _____

How you learned of this book: _____

Reasons why you bought this book: (check all that apply)

□ ATTRACTIVE INSIDE □ RECOMMENDATION OF FRIEND □ SUBJECT □ AUTHOR □ ATTRACTIVE COVER
□ RECOMMENDATION OF REVIEWER □ GIFT

If purchased: Bookseller _____ City _____ State _____

Please send me a SkyLight Paths Publishing catalog. I am particularly interested in: (check all that apply)

1. □ Spirituality
2. □ Mysticism/Meditation
3. □ Philosophy/Theology
4. □ Spiritual Texts
5. □ Religious Traditions (Which ones?)
_____
6. □ Children's Books
7. □ Prayer/Worship
8. □ (Other) _____

Name (PRINT) _____ Phone _____

Street _____ E-mail _____

City _____ State _____ Zip _____

Please send a SkyLight Paths Publishing catalog to my friend:

Name (PRINT) _____ Phone _____

Street _____

City _____ State _____ Zip _____

SkyLight Paths Publishing

Sunset Farm Offices, Rte. 4 • P.O. Box 237 • Woodstock, VT 05091 • Tel: (802) 457-4000 Fax: (802) 457-4004

Available at better booksellers. Visit us online at www.skylightpaths.com

baths to each updated room, replacing communal showers and paving the way for opening the retreat house to women. The community now sets aside two weeks every month for female retreatants, who, from the beginning, have outnumbered their male counterparts. There's almost always a waiting list for "women's weeks" at the retreat house. Like Gethsemani, most monasteries—but not all—open their retreat houses to men and women alike. Specific rules vary from community to community.

At Gethsemani, each retreat room is furnished with a single bed, an easy chair, a desk and desk chair, a nightstand, lamps, and an unforgettable view. The modest private baths have tiled showers. Miniblinds cover the casement windows. Overall, the décor is simple—close to Scandinavian in style—with a certain Spartan charm. Plain wooden crosses and reproductions of icons painted by a Gethsemani monk grace the walls. Windows open out to beautiful views, looking toward either the knobs or the pond inside the monastic enclosure.

Though Gethsemani's retreat house is fairly typical, visitors' quarters vary from monastery to monastery, with some not so well furnished or beautifully situated.

A first encounter with a monastery is not a purely visual experience, however. Far from it. Especially at Gethsemani, there is an aural component that is equally powerful. It is true that guests are encouraged to be silent in the hallways of the retreat house and quiet in their rooms. But there are other sounds. Church bells, for example, ring out the time of day and announce the start of each of the seven daily hours of the *Opus Dei* ("Work of God"). These public liturgical services take place in church and consist of hymns, psalms, canticles, and other prayers. Set out in the Rule of St. Benedict and still followed today by monks all over the world, the hours punctuate the Cistercian's day from 3:15 in the morning to 7:30 at night. The purpose is to praise, thank, and petition God on behalf of the world at large. All monks are expected to

Retreatants in a meditation garden. Retreat house gardens provide peaceful settings for meditation or reading. Visitors often stop here for a few moments of silence after attending Mass or one of the liturgical hours in the church.

be present for each service unless their work requires them to be away.

Tolling bells can also denote other important events in a monastery. A sustained series of tolls indicates that death is at hand for one of the community's monks. It is a call to all his brothers to assemble at his bedside and be present with him in prayer and love as he dies.

Another traditional and characteristic sound of Trappist life is that of chant. During each of the monastic services, the monks gather for what they refer to informally as choir. This refers to the division of the community into two groups, facing one another from opposing pews or stalls. In this formation they chant psalms, verse by verse, back and forth, in response to one another. They chant from a book, called "the Psalter," that contains all the psalms. Booklets in the rear of the public section of the church provide visitors and retreatants with the words and music for each hour. As is true at most Trappist and Benedictine monasteries, retreatants and other visitors are encouraged to participate in Gethsemani's songs and prayers and in its daily Mass.

Though Gregorian chant went out with the use of Latin, following church reforms of the 1960s, a modern version of that unique choral music is used today at Gethsemani and other Catholic monasteries. Trappists traditionally complete a full cycle of 150 psalms every two weeks. Standing in a candlelit church at 3:15 in the morning, listening to—or joining—the chanting monks is one sure way to feel yourself transported to the Middle Ages.

As a retreatant, you are invited to sing along and respond to prayers with the monks, and, if you are Catholic, you are allowed to share in the Eucharist by taking Communion at daily Mass. Your presence at services is not required, but you are welcome to attend all of them, either as respectful observer or full participant.

There are mundane sounds, as well as prayerful ones, that become familiar at Gethsemani: meal bells, for example, or the audiotapes of Trappist lecturers played over speakers in the retreat house dining room. In the monks' dining room, called "the refectory," at the main meal each day, monks listen to one of their brothers read aloud from a book—usually nonfiction, generally a book dealing with some historical, cultural, or spiritual theme.

Among my own favorite sounds at Gethsemani are several that are decidedly secular. Merton, who was a vocal critic of United States involvement in the war in Vietnam, wrote often about the incessant rumble of gunfire during "war games" at Fort Knox, a nearby army post. That rumble is still audible on clear nights at Gethsemani, a reminder that even the peace and tranquility of monastic life is fragile and can be easily disrupted. The howl of coyotes also finds its way to the monastery from the distant hills and woods. Both these sounds resonate with violence and anxiety. They call the listener back to interior silence and encourage reflection on the disquiet that so easily insinuates itself into our hearts.

Gethsemani has its own special flavors and tastes, too. The meals served in the retreat house are created on site by members of the community. Retreatants and monks eat the same daily meals; the only differences are that monks are served smaller portions and no meat. The food is simple fare, befitting Trappist austerity, and it is served, buffet style, to retreatants at a steam table in a small, well-run kitchen. Meals are taken in the retreat house dining room, where all chairs face the same direction—directly toward the floor-to-ceiling windows that look out to the garden, the road beyond it, and even further, to the knobs. No arrangement could be more contemplative-friendly. Visual distractions from passersby or other diners are kept to a minimum, encouraging mindful eating and fostering feelings of gratitude and love.

Of course, there are also distinctive smells associated with Gethsemani. Situated in a rural neighborhood, as Cistercian monasteries tend to be, the air is relatively untainted by industrial pollution or exhaust from heavy traffic. It smells as fresh as the cedar saplings that sprout each year, as comforting as the incense that burns in the church at certain times of prayer.

If you happen to be invited to tour the cloistered areas of the monastery, you might catch a whiff of other typical Gethsemani smells: the pungent aroma of Port du Salut–style cheese aging in refrigerated vaults, for example, or the sweet smell of fudge laced with fine Kentucky bourbon. You may pick up the scent of cakes fresh from the oven, smelling of fruit, spices, and pecans. These are the three lines of popular food products that Gethsemani sells to the public through its mail-order and Internet business, Gethsemani Farms. Like all Trappist monasteries, Gethsemani supports itself by the labor of its monks.

At Holy Trinity Abbey outside Salt Lake City, the Trappist monks sell honey they produce in various flavored spreads. At Our Lady of the Mississippi Abbey in Dubuque, Iowa, Trappists nuns (known as Trappistines) make and sell various kinds of candy. Other monasteries specialize in jellies, jams, bakery products, and even bonsai trees.

Though they represent only a small part of the monastic life, the trappings of a Trappist monastery deliver a powerful first impression. The handmade products, the chant, the bucolic setting, the architecture, the smells and tastes and sounds—all invite a closer look.

Becoming Who We Are

Nothing is expected of us except "to be." That sounds great,
until you have to do it. —A GETHSEMANI MONK

Catholic monasteries tend to have distinct personalities. In the course of a casual visit, you can sense the mood and tone of a community, its attitude toward itself and visitors, the collective voice with which it speaks, silently, to God and to the world.

At Gethsemani, you can pick it up it at 3:15 in the morning in church, at noon in the meditation garden, in the evening on a walk along the avenue. You hear it in the monks' chant, feel it in the way the cup is passed to you at Mass. If you make the trek through the woods to the bronze statues depicting Christ and his disciples in the garden of Gethsemani, you will certainly discern it there.

The personality of Gethsemani is an accepting one, a personality that attracts and welcomes people in spiritual crisis. Perhaps this personality is an outgrowth of the name, Gethsemani, which calls to mind Christ at a critical point in his own spiritual suffering. This is a monastery where people come to hit bottom and start over, as the monks will tell you. "Every abbey has its flavor—that's ours," Brother Christian LeBlanc told me. "Our main purpose is to pray. But a part of our rule also is to have a place where people can come to fall apart."

Supporting outsiders in crisis is part of a monk's job description. I remember meeting a woman close to my own age on my first visit to

Gethsemani. I noticed her sitting outdoors, reading, and praying at night in the church. I finally spoke to her one evening after she finished using the only public telephone in the retreat house, a pay phone off the lobby. I was waiting to make a call of my own to my husband and son at home. Instead, I struck up a conversation with the woman.

She told me how she had been back to Gethsemani four or five times since her first visit the year before during a trying period of hurry-up-and-wait with adoption agencies. She and her husband had been disappointed several times by arrangements that fell through at the last minute. Each visit to Gethsemani seemed to arrive just as she was in need of emotional and spiritual refuge following such a letdown.

At those retreats, she recalled, "I would cry the whole time." She remembered, too, how much Brother Luke Armour, then the guest-master, had helped her through those crises. When she and her husband finally succeeded in adopting, they asked Luke to be the godfather. He couldn't attend the baptismal ceremony but he was there "by proxy," she said. During his tenure as guestmaster, Brother Luke kept a framed baby photo of his godchild on his desk. A decade later, the family still makes regular visits.

"There's a feeling of peace here that I don't feel anywhere else," the new mother told me at our first encounter. With monasteries, as with individuals, a peaceful aura usually signifies an underlying toler-ance and acceptance of others. Part of the appeal of a monastery is that no one expects you to be anyone but who you are. The doubting, the unfaithful, the seekers, the angry, the desperate—all are welcome. This could explain why abbeys like Gethsemani are visited by young and old alike, people of all faiths (and no faith), from all walks of life, from big city and small town.

"My guess is that the culture is so overstimulating that this offers refreshment without rival," Brother Luke said. "There are no expecta-tions here. No place to go and all day to get there."

In church, on a Monday (or any "workday"), you are likely to see the brothers dressed in flannel shirts, jeans, and sneakers. Fewer will be wearing the traditional Cistercian habit, or uniform, of white robes with black scapulars, or aprons, and belts. Later in the day, after their work is done, or very early, before work begins, monks are more likely to wear their habits. During the cooler months of the year, they also wear their cowls—long, hooded, ample-sleeved white cloaks.

What you may not expect to see at a Cistercian monastery, however, is a female monk, dressed in the traditional garb, in choir, chanting psalms with the brothers. Coed Catholic monasteries do not exist. But at Gethsemani, since the mid-1990s, it has not been unusual to see a female Trappist in the midst of the male community.

The first, Sister Catharina Shibuya, a Japanese Trappistine, stayed ten months with the community on extended leave from her monastery. When she left, her place was soon filled by Sister Maricela Garcia, a Mexican nun whose monastery is in the redwoods of northern California. Sister Maricela has lived at Gethsemani, on and off, for several years, with the approval of the abbot general of the order. Her presence has become another sign of the community's welcoming embrace. "I don't see the monks as just a community of men," Sister Maricela said, "but as a community of monastic people with the same issues as women and the same aim—to lead the monastic life."

Day Is Done

I will bless the Lord who gives me counsel, who even at night directs my heart. . . . And so my heart rejoices, and my soul is glad; even my body shall rest in safety.　　　　　　　　　　　—PSALM 16:7, 9

At the close of the day, monks all over the world gather in their churches for the final hour of prayer, called "compline," from the Latin word for "complete." At Gethsemani, as at most abbeys, compline begins at 7:30 PM and lasts about fifteen minutes. It is a favorite end-of-day ritual for retreatants of all faiths. They routinely fill the church for this good-night prayer service. In summer, it's still light at that time in Kentucky, and the church, where the air conditioning is never turned on, bristles with the Ohio Valley's infamous mugginess and heat. In winter, on the other hand, it is pitch dark in rural Nelson County by 7:30. The final service of the day ends in cold candlelight, as the monks sing their bed-time prayer to Mary, the mother of God.

Compline, like the other six services that punctuate a monk's day, is a mixture of spoken prayer, silent meditation, chant, and song. "Give our weary bodies rest from toil, O Lord," the monks pray, "and grant that the seed we have sown this day may yield a rich harvest for eternity." The theme of compline is God's protection and love for us, with sleep and darkness as metaphors for the risks involved in living without awareness of the divine presence. Since the thirteenth century, compline at Cistercian monasteries has traditionally ended with the singing of Salve Regina ("Hail, Holy Queen"), a hymn to Mary.

At the conclusion of that hymn the monks file to the front of the church in two lines from either side of the nave, stopping when they reach the abbot, who stands before them with a sprinkler filled with water that's been blessed. Each monk bows when the abbot sprinkles him with what Catholics call "holy water," then walks back to his seat. When all of the monks have been blessed for the night, the guestmaster opens a small gate that separates the public part of the church from the monastic portion, permitting visitors and retreatants to join the monks in receiving the abbot's blessing.

Most nights after compline, Father Matthew, the retreat house chaplain, gives a talk in the small chapel adjacent to the church. It's an informal gathering that draws anywhere from twenty to fifty people, mostly retreatants, but also folks from what the monks call "the neighborhood." Kelty, a native of Massachusetts who spent years as a hermit in New Guinea and the rural South, usually begins his talks by reading a few poems by his favorite writers (Robert Frost, Gerard Manley Hopkins, and Wendell Berry, to name a few) and then launches into an enlightening and always entertaining exploration of some current event or religious theme. A lively speaker, he often triggers conversations that trickle out onto the abbey porch and continue among visitors late into the night.

Otherwise, after Father Matthew's talk, things quiet down. While guests may stay up for a late-night walk or to read in the retreat house library, the monks—awake since 3 AM—are ready to bed down in their cells. Only those with essential jobs to perform remain awake. Merton, in one of his first published journals, *The Sign of Jonas*, wrote movingly of his own reflections in the post-compline darkness when he held the job of the night watch. Essentially, the job called for checking each building in the monastery to make sure all was safe and sound, and then clocking the time of each checkpoint for fire insurance purposes.

"At eight-fifteen I sit in darkness," Merton writes in *Sign of Jonas*. "I sit in human silence. Then I begin to hear the eloquent night, the night of wet trees, with moonlight rising over the shoulder of the church in a haze of dampness and subsiding heat. The world of this night resounds from heaven to hell with animal eloquence, with the savage innocence of a million unknown creatures."

Surrendering

Like a weaned child at its mother's breast, even so is my soul.

—PSALM 131:2

I remember a balmy night, a year or so after my first retreat, when I was in my room, lying in bed, unable to sleep because of the sound of disconsolate crying outside my window. I don't know how long I had been hearing it before I was conscious of the baleful bleating. Was this the "savage innocence" of Merton's "million unknown creatures"? I wondered. Though I did finally doze off, my sleep was restless and I awoke many times during the night, jarred from fitful dreams by the mournful cries.

I was sure it was the sound of cows crying—but why? As I lay in my bed, wondering, I began to think of the wailing as a collective lament to God sent up by all of us assembled at Gethsemani that week. I remembered the lines from a familiar psalm: "Out of the depths I cry unto to you. O Lord, hear my prayer."

The next morning, to my surprise, I awoke to the sound of silence. The crying was over. Not even a whimper could be heard. At breakfast I asked one of the monks what the commotion had been about, and he explained that what I had heard was the lowing of cows whose calves had been weaned from them earlier in the day. The keening was the sound of their anguish at separation, their desire for reconnection. In a sense I had been right to equate the cries with the words of the psalm.

I have never forgotten the memory of that night, neither the sounds nor the symbolism. The cows in the barn across the road from where I slept were caught up in the agonizing process of surrender—a fundamental Gethsemani experience.

Most nights, however, a deep silence falls across the monastery after compline, both in the public areas and within the cloister. Only the subtler sounds of nature—crickets and cicada in summer, a cold wind in the cedars in winter—interrupt the monks' rest. Peace reigns until the bells begin tolling at 3:00 AM, signaling the community's wake-up call, summoning monks and visitors alike to the first hour of the new day, called vigils.

2

A Space of Liberty: Observing Life Inside the Walls

The contemplative life must provide an area, a space of liberty, of silence, in which possibilities are allowed to surface and new choices—beyond routine choices— become manifest. —THE ASIAN JOURNAL OF THOMAS MERTON

Learning to Listen

Imagine entering a dark church in the middle of the night, your eyelids heavy, your ears doing their best to resist the tolling bells that call you to attention. Depending on the season, you may find the candlelit sanctuary steamy hot or ice-cold. It may be rain that you hear pounding the walls of the church, or a lone mockingbird's concert from a gingko tree in the garden. You take a seat in a wooden pew, and then join in prayer and song with rows and rows of white-robed monks. The darkness fills with thanksgiving and praise. And all of it—every sound and sight—is happening at 3:15 in the morning, the ritual hour of vigils.

The word *vigil* comes to us from the Latin word for "watch." Spoken of in the plural, vigils is the name given to the first liturgical service of a monk's day, a time when the community stands sentinel in the spiritual sense, displaying faith in the face of the dark night. Vigils begins in the

Exterior of the abbey church. The design of this church emphasizes the simplicity for which Trappists are well known. The modern redesign of the entrance to Gethsemani's church and the renovation of its retreat house (windows at left) won national recognition for its architectural excellence.

wee hours, long before dawn, and lasts about forty-five minutes.

And so the second day of my retreat begins this way—in the dark, in the middle of the night. At the end of vigils, most visitors—myself included—return to their beds for another two hours before rising again, in time for the next service, lauds. But for the monk, vigils marks the true start of the day. For him, there is no going back to sleep.

The period of time immediately following vigils is a continuation of what Trappists call the "Grand Silence," when they refrain from speaking. It begins with compline and lasts about twelve hours, until the end of Mass the next morning. It's not a rigid rule, but rather a gentle reminder. It's a lot like the sign in the elevator at the retreat house that requests, not demands, silence in most areas of the building. If you happen to speak to someone in those designated quiet areas, no one will throw you out, or take you to task, or even give you a stern look. But if you keep the atmosphere of silence, doing so will be its own reward. You will find that you are not so much speaking less as hearing more, sensing more, learning more.

Silence, as a monastic value, is less about rejecting speech and more about being attentive and learning to listen—a discipline that could benefit us all. It is not by accident that St. Benedict began his celebrated Rule with the imperative "Listen," not "Be silent." The difference is subtle but significant.

Contrary to popular thinking, in fact, there is no formal "vow of silence." Silence is an important part of St. Benedict's Rule, one of the basic elements of the Benedictine way of life, and highly encouraged. But it more of a value than a vow, more a rule than a promise.

A vow is a solemn pact a monk makes with God, voiced publicly and bestowing serious obligations. Trappists do not make vows hastily: the process leading to a monk's "solemn profession" or "permanent vows" takes an average of six years, though it can last up to nine, and includes a probationary period that is served after making temporary or "simple vows."

Ultimately, Cistercians (and all Benedictines) make three solemn promises: the vow of obedience, which requires a monk to fulfill all that is legitimately asked of him; the vow of stability, a promise to abide by God's call to stay put in his monastery with his brothers; and the vow of conversion of manners, a commitment to remain faithful to the goals of monastic life, which encompasses the traditional vows of poverty and chastity.

Although there is no formal vow of silence, Trappists are expected to use speech sparingly. Depending on their jobs, that's a more difficult goal for some monks than for others. The guestmaster, for example, must be free to carry on conversations with retreatants and other visitors if he is to do his job effectively. To shun conversation with a troubled visitor is hardly a compassionate act. As one Gethsemani brochure puts it, "Silence is not an absolute. Sometimes charity is better served by speaking."

The idea is to listen to all spoken words with respect. That includes the Word of God, the remarks of spiritual leaders, and the speech of all others as well. It's been said that this respect for words inspired the monks of Europe to take on the job of safeguarding the literature of their times, which they did so effectively in the Middle Ages. If it were not for the medieval Christian monks who took that job upon themselves, many of the great works of Western civilization would have been lost.

But the rule of silence, for all its good intentions, was at times considered an end in itself. Prior to the sweeping church reforms of the 1960s, monks were prohibited from speaking directly to one another, even on the job, and certainly from chatting with visitors. As a result, a primitive form of monastic sign language grew up among the monks as a substitute for the spoken word—a system still employed today, in a pinch, by some of the older brothers. But most monks who lived through that period agree that sign language defeated the spirit, if not the letter, of the "law" of silence.

The medieval silence of Thomas Merton's Gethsemani, the life he wrote about so eloquently in his early books, no longer exists. In the 1960s, as gradual changes took place within Catholic monasteries

Monks and bikes. Contrary to the common wisdom, Trappist monks do not take a vow of silence. They follow a rule that emphasizes silence and solitude as a way of leading a contemplative life devoted to God, but conversation is allowed. They take three vows: of stability, or commitment to stay put in one monastery; obedience; and conversion of manners, which includes poverty and chastity.

around the world, monks were given the personal freedom to decide when a conversation was valid and when silence better served the community.

Father Felix Donahue, a monk who entered Gethsemani in 1952 and later became superior of a monastery in the mountains of Brazil, said that the changes "made for a more human kind of community." He recalls being surprised by the personalities of some brothers with whom he had lived for more than a decade. When he began to carry on conversations with them, they contradicted the opinions he had formed over the years, opinions based on observing but rarely communicating with them. "They were quite different people from the images they projected when we were all in silence," he said.

The change from a totally silent to a speaking community also created friendships where they had not existed earlier. In the silent days, individual personal relationships were discouraged. They were viewed as getting in the way of a life of prayer. "Now friendship is encouraged," Father Felix told me during a visit to Gethsemani. "It's [understood as] a way to prayer and to God, not as an obstacle or distraction."

Listening to the Word of God

The fervor and success of a religious order depends entirely on how close it can manage to keep to the object for which it was founded.
— THOMAS MERTON, *THE WATERS OF SILOE*

During the morning hours of the Grand Silence, a monk is likely to set aside time for four ancient monastic spiritual practices. These practices are integral to Benedictine life as well as Cistercian life. The first is sacred reading, known as *lectio divina.* The second is *meditatio,* or meditation, the silent reflection or study that may flow from sacred reading. The third is *oratio,* or prayer. The fourth is *contemplatio,* or contemplation, a deep spiritual silence detached from any thought or image, a state of spiritual receptivity that transcends ordinary consciousness and leads to what St. Gregory the Great called "resting in God."

The term *lectio* is often used to refer to the entire process described above, although the movement from reading to ruminating to praying to "resting in God" is usually not a seamless movement. St. Jerome, a fourth-century monk and scholar, summed up the difference between prayers of, say, thanksgiving or praise and the prayer that comes out of the practice of *lectio* this way: "If you pray, you are speaking to your Lord; if you read, God is speaking to you."

Lectio, of all the elements of monastic life, is most likely to confuse an outsider. This may be because it is a practice based entirely on faith, aimed at achieving a goal that is almost indescribable, even by those who attain it regularly. According to Dom Bernardo Olivera, abbot general of the Cistercian order worldwide, "*Lectio* is not, as a rule, immediately gratifying. It is an active and passive process of long duration. One does not reap the day after sowing!"

Perhaps because *lectio* is an ongoing process that requires patience and perseverance, St. Benedict, in his Rule, assigned many hours of daily *lectio* to his monks. He was explicit about the time and degree of attention they were to devote to this essential monastic practice. Benedict went so far as to dictate precise reading schedules for his men. He even specified the rooms where *lectio* was allowed during the different liturgical seasons of the year.

From spring to fall, for example, monks were permitted to read, discreetly, while resting on their dormitory beds after the noon meal. "Should a brother wish to read privately," Benedict wrote, "let him do so, but without disturbing the others."

At the beginning of Lent, the Rule called for each monk to receive a special book from the library and "to read the whole of it straight through." This practice continues today. At Gethsemani, books are distributed on the first Sunday of Lent and read daily at a special time allotted for that purpose, between the evening meal and compline.

Just in case a monk missed Benedict's point about *lectio*, the Rule also called for one or two senior monks to make the rounds of the monastery during reading time. "Their duty," wrote Benedict, "is to see that no brother is so apathetic as to waste time or engage in idle talk to the neglect of his reading, and so not only harm himself but also distract others." On Sundays, any monk who was not assigned a job for the day was expected to be reading. Benedict took no prisoners on this issue: a monk found "remiss or indolent" about his *lectio* was to be given a job to perform, on the spot.

Lectio traditionally referred to reading passages from Scripture, biblical commentaries, and other writings on the spiritual life by the early Christian authors who are sometimes called "the church fathers" (or "elders"). Today, monks define *lectio* more broadly, interpreting it to include reflective reading of other material suitable for spiritual enrichment. Other kinds of books are helpful, according to the abbot general, Dom Bernardo, in that they "allow us to assimilate the Mystery and be transformed by it."

Brother Raphael Prendergast, a monk of Gethsemani since 1954, described *lectio* to me as "reading with the expectancy that some word, phrase, paragraph, or page is worth stopping and reflecting on—a message that fits somewhere in our search."

Like most of us, monks today read all kinds of books. Unlike the old days, when monasteries controlled and censored their monks' reading material, Trappists at Gethsemani read what they wish. In addition to reflecting on passages from the Bible or works of a spiritual nature, they might tackle the biography of Mother Teresa or some international political activist. They might read a novel, classic or contemporary, that explores its characters' moral conflicts. The point of *lectio*, regardless of the subject matter, is to listen to what one is reading with "the ear of the heart."

Make no mistake about it—this kind of reading is far different from simple information gathering, and it is taught as a discipline to monks-in-training. It is neither intellectual nor emotional. Its goal is to open up the reader to God's voice between the lines. Even its translation as "sacred reading" can be misleading, as Dom Bernardo noted in a letter on *lectio* circulated to all Cistercian monks and nuns in 1993: "*Lectio* differs from spiritual reading. While spiritual reading can have as its end the acquisition of knowledge, the formulation of convictions, or the stimulus for generous self-giving, the aim of [*lectio*] is union with God in faith and love."

Resting with the Word

Meditatio, on the other hand, is an active rumination on a passage, a further study and reflection that flows out of *lectio*. It's designed to deepen a monk's concentration and awareness of what he has read and ultimately bring him closer to God. It encompasses a variety of activities, including memorizing and reciting passages or phrases from a text or simply letting images arise while lingering on a line from Scripture.

"To meditate is to chew and ruminate, for it is to repeat, reflect, remember, interpret, penetrate," Dom Bernardo wrote. And what is the goal of the process? How does one know when that goal has been reached? The abbot general's answer is at once simple and enigmatic: "When the text speaks to your heart, you have reached and received a precious fruit of meditation."

Such meditations may well lead the monk to voice, vocally or silently, a personal prayer, which is called *oratio*. It may take the form of a spontaneous prayer of gratitude and praise, or it may surface as a heartfelt petition or confession to God. Or it may induce a profound silence.

Ideally, it leads to *contemplatio*, the prayerful union with God that is the object of monastic life. Rather than viewing this pinnacle of *lectio* as an act of will or the result of technical mastery, contemplatives consider it a gift. In contemplative prayer, inside or outside of the monastery, the only "method" or "technique" involved is surrendering oneself in silence to the presence of God. "In other words, the true contemplative is not the one who prepares his mind for a particular message that he wants or expects to hear," Merton wrote in his book *Contemplative Prayer*, "but who remains empty because he knows that he can never expect or anticipate the word that will transform his darkness into light."

One Benedictine nun, writing about *lectio* on a Benedictine Internet website, defined contemplation as "both a relaxation of our faculties and their total alertness." She described it as "the Lord praying in us rather than our prayer. It is God unifying our entire being at the very center, 'in the cave of the heart,' as the Eastern writers liked to say."

At most monasteries the process of *lectio* comes in as many forms as there are monks. Individuals mix and match the elements of this continuum of prayer throughout their day, depending on what else is expected of them. At Gethsemani, some may start the morning with sacred reading—verses from Scripture, or a passage from a Catholic author—that leads them right into contemplation. Or they may linger over their responses to the reading during breaks from wrapping fruitcakes or taking phone orders for cheese. They may silently, throughout the day, find their responses turning into prayers as they sweep a kitchen floor, drive a pickup truck into town for supplies, or walk from a toolshed on one side of the monastery to a broken pipe on the other. They may close the day in the dark of their cells with more prayer, more reading, or, God willing, more contemplation. Combined with the formal hours of chanting in church and praying at morning Mass, this is the true rhythm of a monk's day.

Outside the monastery, in lay Christian circles, a modified version of *lectio divina* goes by the names of "centering prayer," "prayer of the heart," or "sitting meditation." Father Thomas Keating, a Cistercian monk of St. Benedict's Monastery in Snowmass, Colorado, is a leading advocate of the centering prayer movement and a founder of Contemplative Outreach, an organization dedicated to promoting contemplative prayer outside monastic walls.

Sister Mary Margaret Funk, a Benedictine nun and another leading figure in the centering prayer movement, has described monastic life this way: "Our work is our prayer, and our prayer is our work." For the average visitor, this balance is clearly the major distinction between life in a monastery and life outside it. The monk's life is one that is specifically designed to allow for an almost seamless interaction of prayer, reading, and work.

Staying Put

Find the place that God has given you and take root there. The ability to stand firm, to be where you are and to dwell with oneself is a sign of maturity of mind. This is stability.

—FROM THOMAS MERTON'S MONASTIC CONFERENCES AT GETHSEMANI

In the hours before dawn, then, the monk finds the time and space to be present to God with few distractions. Unlike those of us outside the enclosure, he is not besieged by morning traffic reports or gruesome headlines at the breakfast table. Monks don't have children to feed, mortgages to pay, spouses who are battling cancer, or job discrimination. While their lives are not carefree (they too have deadlines to meet at their jobs), they live in a community that affirms and nourishes the basic spiritual impulses that the outside world tends to repress. "My experience is that monks don't find it any easier to pray than anyone else," a Trappist once told me. "But we have structure to support and encourage it."

On the other hand, community life has its own pressures and strains. The monk doesn't have a choice about who sleeps in the room next to his or who chants beside him in church. He has no say about who eats at the place beside him at the dinner table every night. He takes his place chronologically, according to the date he entered the monastery. That element of community life—adjusting to living with a house full of strangers—can be one of the toughest challenges a monk faces.

This is, after all, a lifetime commitment for Cistercian monks. The vow of stability requires a monk not only to promise to remain a member of the order, but also to remain a monk in the very monastery where he took his vows, and to refrain from seeking other communities that perhaps seem more congenial. It is a decision to limit oneself voluntarily to one group of people, staying put to work out the problems that

Exterior of south wing of Our Lady of Gethsemani Monastery. The abbot's office is located on the first floor of the south wing of the monastery. The monks' private rooms are on the second and third floors.

arise rather than escaping when the going gets rough. Obviously, this position is a radical departure from the mobility and lack of rootedness in our culture at large.

The vow of conversion of manners, or fidelity, demands another kind of surrendering to community—a willingness to turn yourself over to the good of a community and allow yourself to be shaped by your relationship to your brothers. This requires giving up a certain degree of individuality and autonomy. It means stopping whatever you're doing at the toll of a bell, no matter how inconvenient; listening to others when you would rather not; sticking with difficult relationships even when they become tiresome or seem fruitless. It's a way of life that demands discipline and an authentic spiritual commitment.

And, oh yes, it helps to have a sense of humor as well, according to Gethsemani's abbot, Father Damien Thompson. In his office in the south wing of the monastery, on a sunny day a few weeks after his brothers elected him to the highest office at the abbey in the spring of 2000, Father Damien described the dilemma of community life in his characteristically straightforward fashion. Where St. Benedict wrote about community life in formal and exacting terms befitting the times, Father Damien tackles the subjects with an attitude that is more practical and down-to-earth, and certainly more attuned to modern realities.

"You see, here you don't choose the people you're with. We joke about it—you wouldn't even want to go out and have a beer with most of these guys," he laughed.

Father Damien was a priest for seventeen years before entering Gethsemani in 1978 at the age of forty-five. While a member of the Maryknoll Catholic Foreign Mission Society he served as a fundraiser and recruiter in schools and parishes in New Orleans and Philadelphia. During a midlife hiatus from the priesthood in the 1970s he held a series of non-religious jobs, ranging from stints as a legal aid investigator and equal-opportunity officer for the city of Chicago to driving a taxi. At Gethsemani his posts have included guestmaster, baker, kitchen boss, and prior, which is the "vice-abbot" job at an abbey. The prior takes over when the abbot is out of town, making weekly "chapter talks" to the community and running the house.

As abbot, Father Damien follows Father Timothy Kelly, a Canadian priest who chose to retire from the post after running the house for a dynamic twenty-seven-year tenure. The two men come across very differently in conversation. Father Timothy, who still carries a slight Canadian accent, is smaller, quieter, and more reserved than his affable successor.

When the conversation in Father Damien's office turned to community life, he told me he believes God works "a miracle" in monasteries when he "throws together" groups of men or women who, if it were up to them, would never volunteer to live together, even for a year or two.

"Outside, sure, you may struggle with relationships, but you're struggling with people you love, or with friends you've chosen," Father Damien said. "Here, you haven't chosen. It's a conglomeration of folks from all over the country. But God says, 'I'm going to work a miracle.' And he does. Something happens in the process."

What happens is that strangers become a community—an inspiration and a support to one another along the spiritual path. Father Damien said that his twenty-two years at Gethsemani have honed his ability to bond to people. He feels it in his relationships with fellow monks as well as with visitors he encounters day to day. And yet, he acknowledges that "younger guys" sometimes struggle with what they consider to be a lack of satisfying relationships in the monastery or, even more frustrating, their inability to get along with some of their brothers. "They say, 'I don't have relationships here. I wonder if it's even possible. You can't relate to just anybody,'" Father Damien said. Then he shrugged his shoulders. "But somehow you do. You end up with good relationships."

The Perfect Monk

Father Damien believes that a monk's difficulties with community life are often a result of immaturity and lack of experience. Men who are older when they enter the monastic life have had time to live on their own, support themselves, develop careers, and forge strong friendships before opting for communal life. Compared to younger monks, they may have earned greater insight about themselves and may feel more comfortable about their emotional responses—positive and negative—to other people.

Sitting in a chair by his office window, Father Damien smiled and slowly rubbed the palm of one hand back and forth across his chin as if listening to a voice inside his own head. "I mean, for me, I love monastic life. I can do my spiritual life the way I want to do it. Something happens when you are given a chunk of time, and you are told 'Hey, this is yours.' A blank space of time. You see, life gets fatter. Each moment is fatter." He paused and then smiled. "I can live in the fat of the moment."

He said he is grateful to be at this stage of his life and spiritual journey. He was not always so relaxed or comfortable with his role as a cloistered monk or, before that, as a priest in active community service. To illustrate his point, he told a story from his early years at Gethsemani, when he was striving to be, as he put it, "the perfect monk."

By his own account, at the time he took his solemn vows, Father Damien had established a detailed schedule for each day of the week to make sure he balanced his prayer, work, and reading lives. When he was immediately appointed guestmaster—one of the most public and noncontemplative jobs at the monastery—he balked. He worried that running the retreat house would take time and energy away from his spiritual reading and prayer. He knew it was an unpredictable job, one that could easily throw his "schedule" into disarray. "I had it mechanized. And being guestmaster would mess up my little system," he said, smiling at the memory. "I had to figure out my whole day. Everything had to be equal. I was anxious about it, you know. I was trying to become the perfect monk."

He feared what might happen if he took the job, but ultimately he surrendered those fears to God. Soon, he realized that the job actually enriched his spiritual life. He met visitors who challenged and inspired him. What's more, he seemed to be left with as much time as he needed to pray and to read, too. "Within a couple of weeks, I realized the important thing was to be in the present, just to be in the present with each person I met—to make prayer of my work," he said. "Each job I've had since then, I've had an insight like that."

The fundamental discipline in a monastery is obedience, Father Damien said. In monastic terms, obedience does not mean blind submissiveness, but rather, implies an act of surrendering the will to God and being open to the prompting of spiritual guides. It's not an abdication of personal responsibility but an acceptance of the need to discern what God wants of you, often with the help of another person who has your best spiritual interests at heart. "Our preconceptions are what screw us up—even about holiness," Father Damien said. "You know, you come in here with an idea of the kind of person you want to become, and then when that doesn't happen you become dissatisfied with who you are. 'I don't like it because it doesn't fit in with my preconceptions.' But you have to adjust."

Father Damien shook his head. Perhaps he was thinking of his own experience as a young monk or remembering a tale told to him by a brother. Certainly the stories are legion about monks who struggled for years and found peace with life at Gethsemani only when they gave up the romantic notion of the ideal community, the model monk, the perfect prayer life. They came to terms with their brothers only after they learned to accept and to love themselves, warts and all.

Over the years I have filled scores of notebooks with bits of conversation recorded, overheard, or engaged in at Gethsemani. One of my favorites is this description, by a monk, of the challenge of community life: "Survival here is about knowing yourself and accepting yourself. And the other half of that coin is knowing and accepting everybody else."

On my very first visit to Gethsemani, I had asked a monk to describe what life was like for him and his brothers. "God is teaching us who we are here," he said, "and that's mysterious."

This is the job all of us face, inside or outside cloistered walls: discovering who we are. As monks, there's more to it than simply the discovery, however. There is the personal response that must flow out from that knowledge, back to God. As Father Damien summed it up for me that day in his office, "You have to learn to praise God for who you are."

Reaching Out

The contemplative life should not be regarded as the exclusive pre-
rogative of those who dwell within monastic walls. All men can seek
and find this infinite awareness and awakening.
—FROM THOMAS MERTON'S MONASTIC CONFERENCES AT GETHSEMANI

There are lots of jokes about "monastic time." The punch lines invariably focus on how unconcerned monks are about the deadlines and
agendas that tend to dominate the waking hours of the rest of humankind. But it's really no joke. When you spend time at a monastery as a
visitor or retreatant, it's true that you lose track of the world's rhythms
and find yourself tapping into a less rigid, more natural, tempo.

This is what contemplative life "feels like" to both the monk who lives
it and the guest who dips into it from time to time. It is what lures so
many men and women to the retreat houses of monasteries—Trappists
and other Benedictines alike—and what has fueled the growing interest among Americans in all things monastic, even as they spend more
and more time tethered to cell phones and stock tables.

It is what Father Damien means when he speaks of "fat time" and
being present to the moment. It is what the Rule of St. Benedict sets out
to preserve. It is what motivates 9,096 men and 18,200 women to voluntarily live under that Rule in Benedictine monasteries, and it is what
inspires growing numbers of men and women who don't live in monasteries to integrate its precepts into their daily routines, formally or
informally.

Before he became the superior of a monastery in Brazil in the early
1990s, Father Felix Donahue spent several years as guestmaster at Gethsemani. His experience with retreatants convinced him that Benedictine
hospitality is a two-way street. A soft-spoken, articulate monk, Father
Felix said that the monastery receives as much as it gets when it welcomes

visitors. "When these people come here for a week or longer, we know they don't have to do that," he said. "They've got other things to do at home and at work. Nobody makes them get up at three for vigils or turn out for Mass or keep reasonably quiet. But they do it. So their very presence feeds back, I feel, to our community, and we gain by the example of these busy people, parents and professionals, who make time to spend the weekend or a whole week at a monastery. I receive life from these people."

Most monks don't spend time with visitors or retreatants. They only observe them in church or in the woods, perhaps, when their paths cross. But Father Felix contends that the constant presence of visitors at Gethsemani—seekers and sightseers alike—speaks volumes to the monks who live there.

The next question, then, is, What does the visitor take away from an encounter with a monastic community? Father Felix thinks he understands that side of the equation too. "There are certain things that resonate for people who come here," he said. "There are elements in our monastic life and spirituality that speak to them. There may be something they connect with and feel they could incorporate into their own lives perhaps. Things like a balance between work and leisure. People time and personal time. Time to reflect, to digest, to worship."

Living Like a Monk

Certainly, Michael Brown would agree with Father Felix on that score. Brown, who briefly tried out the monastic life at Gethsemani in the early 1970s, is now part of a group he helped organize called Cistercian Lay Contemplatives, or CLC. Its members meet monthly for prayer and conversation, either at the monastery or at the Thomas Merton Center on the campus of Bellarmine College in Louisville. Most, like Brown, had some prior connection to monasticism, even if only through reading about it in the works of Merton.

Brown told me, "My relationship with the monastery began around 1970, when I made my first retreat." At the time, he was a postulant, or probationary candidate, in another religious order. The retreat convinced him, however, that his true spiritual home was Gethsemani. He entered the community in 1972 but only stayed a year "for reasons," he said, "that are still not clear to me, even to this day." Brown adds, "I like to think I was a seed which germinated in the monastery and then was blown by the Spirit back into the world. When I left, I had no idea I would become part of a worldwide lay contemplative movement."

When he left, he did feel certain, however, that he would continue the prayer life he had begun as a novice at Gethsemani. Even after he married and started a family, Brown prayed the liturgy of the hours daily, as the monks do, and continued to read contemplative writers.

Eventually, he began to practice centering prayer, the lay version of *lectio* that Father Thomas Keating advocates through the organization he helped establish, Contemplative Outreach. Then, in the late 1980s, a friend introduced him to Mike Johnson of Cincinnati, a man who shared Brown's enthusiasm for incorporating elements of monastic life into secular life. Over the next few years the two met at Gethsemani several times with a small group of like-minded souls and eventually wrote a lay version of St. Benedict's Rule, which they called "Plan of Life." Among other things, it calls for those who follow it to spend at least thirty minutes a day in quiet prayer and meditation, preferably half that time in the morning and half in the evening.

Father Michael Casagram, a former vocations director at Gethsemani, worked with the group as they began to attract members from beyond Kentucky. Early on, members of the group chose the name Cistercian Lay Contemplatives and began referring to their fledgling organization as CLC.

Today, CLC publishes a newsletter, has a membership of about 150 people from thirty-four states and Canada, and sponsors a yearly group retreat at Gethsemani, often a joint venture of the Louisville and Cincinnati groups. Brown estimates there are hundreds of people across the country who are connected, informally, to Cistercian monasteries like Gethsemani. In 1999, with the help of Father Basil Pennington, another Trappist monk and author, the CLC drafted a constitution of its own. Entitled "Bond of Charity," it is modeled after the original Cistercian constitution, which is known as the "Charter of Charity."

Unlike Benedictine monks and nuns, Cistercians, as an order, do not formally recognize "oblates" or "third orders," the traditional names given to lay people who choose to live in close connection to a monastery. Two daughter houses, or spin-off monasteries, of Gethsemani—one in New York and one in Georgia—have formed somewhat official ties with lay groups. But such alliances are rare. "I think the order is struggling with what to do with us," Brown said. "The Trappists are a cloistered order. The lay groups respect that, but they still feel an attraction and a desire to share Cistercian spirituality."

What kind of person wants to take up the challenge of living the monastic life in the secular world? Some are like Brown, former Trappist postulants or novices who did not want to give up the prayer life and peace they tasted while in the monastery. Others are newcomers to monastic spirituality. They may have only read about it, or maybe dipped into it on a retreat. Some live within walking distance of monasteries. Others live nowhere near one. They are young and old, male and female, but they do tend to be mostly white and predominantly middle-class. "Most are people who are deeply spiritual, and sometimes they are active in their parishes," Brown said. "But more than a few feel on the fringe of parish life, which typically doesn't provide them the depth of spirituality they are seeking. I would say most are well-educated, though not all are professionals."

People like Brown and Bea Keller, a past coordinator of Kentucky's

Contemplative Outreach, are attempting to build bridges between the religious vows of monks and the spiritual yearnings of mainstream folks. Contemplative Outreach has active chapters across the country and sponsors several workshops on centering prayer each month, at locations from coast to coast.

A Counterpoint to the World

But why the burgeoning interest in all things monastic at this particular point in time? St. Benedict's Rule was written, after all, at a time when society seemed to be falling apart. Its appeal to men and women of that chaotic time was as an alternative, a discipline, a counterpoint to the corroding values and crumbling political alliances of the era.

Today, we may feel anxious and overwhelmed for other reasons. The desire to balance our lives and to seek a reality that is more substantial than the Dow Jones Average may be driving more of us to look to less hectic lifestyles for guidance. As Brown also suggested, established congregations and traditional parish life may not be enough for many of today's believers. They seek a more deeply spiritual or mystical element than they can find at their neighborhood church.

Centering prayer is, of course, a way of combining Christian contemplative tradition with a contemporary need to let go of the analytical, technology-driven, superlogical, ultralinear, overactive modern mind. Books on the subject sell faster than bookstores can stock them. Authors like Keating and Pennington, Kathleen Norris and Thomas Moore, have their fans and imitators. Even the Internet is swamped with "dotcoms" devoted to spreading the word (and selling the trappings) of contemplative life.

This isn't exactly a brand-new phenomenon. Two great waves of enthusiasm for monastic life swept across the twentieth century. The first came in the 1940s in conjunction with the disappointment and disillusionment of men returning from World War II. The contrast between the ideals many veterans fought to uphold and the postwar materialistic culture they came home to prompted some to search for alternative lifestyles. Many ended up at monasteries.

The second big wave arrived on the heels of the civil rights, peace and hippie-commune movements of the 1960s and 1970s. At Gethsemani, as at other monasteries around the country, groups of young men and women who wanted to pursue a simple, peaceful, communal lifestyle often showed up at the gatehouses of monasteries, seeking the guidance and experience of the monks who lived there.

Brother Frederic Collins, who worked for Prudential Life Insurance Company and Ford Motor Company before entering Gethsemani in 1954, was the monk who answered the door when the knock came at Gethsemani. A young man named Jim Grote was one of those who knocked. Today, nearly thirty years later, Brother Frederic is the abbey's treasurer. Jim Grote, the author of a recent book on integrating spiritual practice into office management, lives with his family in Louisville.

For several years in the 1970s, however, the two men lived within a few miles of each other. With Brother Frederic's help and support, Grote, with his wife and a group of friends, formed the Families of St. Benedict, a community of spiritually motivated individuals who took up residence on a 105-acre farm near the abbey. The monks, in general, didn't take to the idea of formally associating with the group, perhaps out of fear of being linked to a "hippie commune" whose underlying convictions seemed unclear. In the end, the Families of St. Benedict kept Cistercian rules and rituals as closely as possible for a group that included married and single people, as well as children. They based their life together on monastic principles of communal prayer, voluntary poverty, and contemplation. Over time, some thirty individuals lived on the farm. After a dozen years, the community disbanded and moved on. But many, like Grote, still feel connected to the abbey's spiritual rhythms and often show up for vespers or compline or to visit with their old friends in the community.

Though no other group has bonded to the monastery in quite the same way, individuals and groups have always—and will always—form close relationships to the monastic communities and to the spirit of the life there.

It's true that some visitors look at monks and see only the great gulf of differences that exist between themselves and these cloistered men. But Father Felix, the former guestmaster, thinks that most people identify with some aspect of community life—real or ideal—if they are honest with themselves about it. "I think it's important to keep building bridges between religious life and the laity, instead of persisting in thinking that a religious life is something qualitatively different," he said. "Really, all Christians are basically trying to reach the same goals. I see more continuity than contrast between what we're doing and what the people who come here are doing."

More than fifty years ago, Jack Ford made his first visit to Gethsemani. A Louisville educator, Ford was at first in awe of the silent, prayerful world he discovered there. He considered his own life, as a college professor and family man, to be in a different league. The two lifestyles might complement each other but never intersect in any significant way, he believed.

Ford maintained his ties to Gethsemani over the course of half a century, through the tenures of several abbots. Eventually his views changed, and he stopped believing in a rigid delineation between the "monastic way" on the one hand, and the "lay way" on the other. The Cistercian reforms of the 1960s, prompted by the Catholic church's Second Vatican Council, made it clearer that the two paths had more in common than in opposition. "I don't dispute that we have different vocations," Ford told me, "but at the same time I see more common movement and interest and sharing than I would have ever suspected."

3

The Less-Traveled Road: What It's Like to Become a Monk

By seeking God you have already found him.

—THOMAS MERTON

Morning Has Broken

It's 5:45 AM on the third day of my retreat. Vigils, that interlude of prayer that comes in the dark of night, is now a memory. The monks' early morning hours of reading, reflection, and silent prayer are drawing to a close. The boisterous song of whippoorwills in the meditation garden fades, replaced by the tolling of bells, calling us back to church for lauds, the second hour of the monastic day.

As I head out from my room I wonder again: What brings a man to a monastery? What voice won't let him rest until he finds his way here? Once here, who decides if he's made of the right stuff for solitude and silence? What tests qualify him to stay put at a place like Gethsemani?

These questions stay with me through lauds, the hour whose name means "praise" in Latin. Its arrival at dawn links it to a time of day that, for Christians, symbolizes rebirth and renewal. To believers, daybreak not only ushers in a new day, but also calls to mind the Easter morning resurrection of Christ.

For monks, lauds is a morning ritual of rededication and preparation, a prologue to all that will follow in the course of the day. At Gethsemani, it is one of the longest services, lasting about twenty-five minutes. It includes the chanting of psalms, the singing of hymns, silent and vocal prayers, as well as Bible readings. It begins, as all hours except vigils do, when a second round of tolling bells resounds through the church.

The first tolling of bells is a summons, calling the community and visitors to church. When the bells ring again, five minutes later, the monks rise and turn toward the front of the church to chant the opening of the service.

At lauds I sit in a wobbly wooden pew behind a clear-glass gate that separates monks from visitors. At Mass, which follows immediately on the heels of lauds (except on Sundays, when it begins later), the public will be welcomed up the long center aisle to the metal and plastic chairs arranged in rows near the altar. The monks will move, too, from their stalls to a semicircle of chairs set up even closer to the altar in an area known as the sanctuary. On either side of the sanctuary more chairs are lined up against the walls. Here, the older monks of the community, including some in wheelchairs and on electric scooters, take their places.

Some monasteries have done away with all physical barriers between the community and the outside world in their churches. Monks and public mingle in the same space. But I don't mind the separation at Gethsemani. In fact, I view it as a bittersweet but useful reminder of the less-traveled path that the monk elects to follow when he enters a monastery.

Monks choose seclusion because it is a more fertile medium for breeding interior silence, the necessary ingredient for achieving a contemplative state, or union with God, in prayer. Monks leave behind their possessions and assumptions and come to a place where everything is owned in common and each person is viewed not so much as an individual, but as a unique part of a united whole. Dressed alike, chanting the same 150 psalms twenty-five times over in the course of a year, the monks of Gethsemani seek meaning in tradition and ritual. Going "deep" rather than far afield is the point of their life. The incessant search for "something new" may be the goal of other people in other places, but not here in this church at this hour.

One Monk's Journey

Still, the questions haunt me: What kind of man opts for a life of such detachment and solitude? Does it take a reclusive personality? An indifferent attitude toward relationships and the things of the world? A lack of interest in the culture at large? Must he be an introvert? A hermit? A saint?

The answer clearly is "none of the above." There are, and always have been, extroverts and team players in monasteries, and more than a few wags and wise guys.

I remember settling down for an unhurried chat one afternoon with Father Matthew, Gethsemani's Boston Irish retreat chaplain. At eighty-five, he is a sly and witty conversationalist, a natural storyteller who spices his tales with dramatic gesturing and a standup comic's sense of timing. That day, as I was setting up my tape recorder in his book-laden office on the first floor of the retreat house, Father Matthew watched my every move, smiling benignly. When I finally snapped the record button in place and popped him my first question, "Could you tell me how you got here?" he quipped, "Oh, by Greyhound, I think."

Then he leaned forward in his chair, hiking his robe high enough to reveal his leather cowboy boots, and told me a story that added one more piece to the puzzle of why a man leaves the world and becomes

a monk. Father Matthew was already a priest when he arrived at Gethsemani, and hardly a young man. He had spent years in a seminary and
years after that at the work he was assigned to perform, willingly, wherever it took him. But God wanted something more of him, and Father
Matthew knew it.

Father Matthew said, "I was forty-five when I entered. I was a Divine
Word Missionary. I had always had an interest in monastic life, but it
just never developed." He remembered expressing that interest when
he was in college and in seminary, studying to become a priest. The
response was always, "Oh no, you would never make a monk." His superiors in the mission order told him, "We need you. We can't let you go."

In December of 1959, faced with an unusual stretch of down time
in his work schedule, Father Matthew signed up for a weekend retreat
at Gethsemani, a monastery he had heard of through the work of
Thomas Merton. At the end of the weekend Father Matthew found himself reluctant to leave. Looking back, he says it's clear that the place
was working on him, reawakening and strengthening the desire he had
felt for years but shrugged off. With the blessing of the guestmaster at
Gethsemani, Father Matthew stayed on a few extra days.

"I finally got up enough nerve to ask if I could enter," he said. What
followed was a series of fifteen-minute sessions with members of the
community. The first meeting was with Merton, the novicemaster at the
time; next came a conversation with Father John Eudes Bamberger, a
Gethsemani monk who was also a psychiatrist; the final meeting was
with the abbot of that era, Dom James Fox. ("Dom" was the honorific
applied to Trappist abbots prior to the 1970s; later abbots have opted
for the simpler title of "Father.")

"It was all rather brief and casual," Father Matthew recalled. "And
they said, 'Okay.' All I had to do was send in some papers. The technical stuff. And that's what I did when I got home." A few months later
he entered Gethsemani as a postulant, the first step toward becoming a

monk. But his arrival was delayed by two traumatic and unforgettable events that crossed his path.

The first occurred when he returned home after his visit to Gethsemani. Late one night a nearby building caught fire. In a rush to escape the flames, Father Matthew seared the sole of one foot. He was forced to wait for the burns to heal before he could make the trek to Gethsemani to begin his monastic studies.

It was winter when he was finally well enough to travel. He was on his way back from a trip to Wisconsin one night when the train he was riding hit a truck. He was asked to step out into a winter storm and administer to three men who lay in heaps on the side of the track. It turned out that he was too late to lend physical assistance to the accident victims. All he could do was tend to their spiritual needs, blessing them with bloodstained snow he scooped from the shoulder of the road. A few days after the accident he left on the night train for Gethsemani.

Father Matthew still remembers those vivid images of fire and ice and blood. They have fused into a metaphor for the life he would soon begin: a life of extremes lived in the service of God and other people.

But what was it about Gethsemani, I asked Father Matthew, that made him want to be there in particular rather than some other monastery? He squinted his eyes and stared past me, as if trying to see again what he saw forty years ago when he first glimpsed Gethsemani. "Well, it wasn't the place, because it was not very attractive then, not as it is today. In those days it was dingy, dark, and relatively dirty—like an old tenement," he said, laughing.

It was the "spirit" of Gethsemani that drew him in, he said. Watching the monks from the church balcony, or gallery, as it was called then, Father Matthew fell under the spell of the middle-of-the-night prayers, the medieval robes, the chant, the incense, the songs, the silence, the peace, the absence of aggression and competitiveness.

Another monk, much younger than Father Matthew, once told me that all the romantic trappings are "God's trick" to stir a man's interest. Later, when the going gets rough, it is the memory of that first-blush attraction that keeps a man from turning away, giving up, looking for something easier. It's not so different, in some ways, he said, from falling in love and marrying. When Father Matthew entered Gethsemani that February, the class of monks-in-training that he joined was small. There were only a dozen novices, including several who, like Father Matthew, were ordained priests who had been members of other Catholic religious orders when they heard the call to the monastic life. There were also a couple of college students, a man with a high-level position in the automotive industry, a Native American from Michigan, and a kid fresh out of high school, he recalled. "It was a good mix. There were some very young, and some relatively mature, people. I was probably the oldest," he said.

From the start, Father Matthew—a poet and published essayist who humbly admits only to having "a flair with words"—was drawn to the physical imagery of Trappist life. He was taken by its stark contrasts with the broader American cultural landscape, which was at that time growing increasingly materialistic and ostentatious.

"Here was a bunch of able-bodied men, you know, singing songs and making fruitcake," he said, smiling at the memory. "The life was different then. More grim. More intense. More tough. More difficult. You drank out of tin cups. You just dipped your cup into a common pot of coffee. The food wasn't all that great. The buildings weren't heated. You had no private rooms. In the dormitories, in winter, the windows were covered with frost. And it smelled like a dog coming out of the rain because of all the wool we wore. There was always this strange mixture of incense and wet wool, and oh, maybe a little Pine-Sol, which gave a peculiar fragrance."

Father Matthew had no doubts, once inside Gethsemani, that this was the life for him. "Despite the grimness there was this spirit of camaraderie," he recalled. "A bonding." Later, the strict poverty of the place and the absolute silence would give way to modernizing influences. The grim, dirty, old-fashioned buildings would be updated, renovated, refurbished. But the sense of brotherhood, of men working and praying together for the love of God, would remain for Father Matthew the main attraction, his reason for being a monk.

Leaving the World Behind

In 1954, six years before Father Matthew entered Gethsemani, a World War II veteran from St. Louis came to a similar decision about his life. During the war Paul Prendergast served his country as a naval aviator in the Marine Air Corps. After the war he went to work in the construction business at a time when a nationwide building boom was making men like him, who had grown up during the Depression, richer than they ever dreamed.

Yet, something about the direction of his life didn't feel right to him. He was disturbed by the idea that to be considered successful, he had to earn a certain amount of money, drive a certain kind of car, hold a certain type of job. During the war he believed he was called to defend values that were threatened by outside forces. Now, in the postwar years, he sensed that those same values were being undermined from within the culture.

One night, on Miami Beach, he experienced a personal epiphany—no fireworks or disembodied voices telling him what to do next, but a revelation nevertheless. It was a "deep experience" that he claims forever changed his life and was responsible, ultimately, for his decision to enter Gethsemani and take on a new name: Brother Raphael.

"On Miami Beach out near the water there's a street called Collins Avenue," Brother Raphael recalled. "In those days it was like one long

Cadillac. Each side of that street was marked by small hotels and large hotels and apartments, all of them painted in pastel colors with pastel lights coming on at night. It was a wonderland, a fairyland, to walk along."

As he strolled the beach, he thought about his future, the social scene unfolding around him, the possibility of marriage and raising a family. He was upbeat, optimistic. Who wouldn't be?

"Just on the other side of the hotels was the surf of the Atlantic. You could hear that sloshing in and sloshing out as you walked. I thought to myself, 'Boy this is it.'"

And that's when it happened: "Before my foot hit the pavement again, it all turned to muck." The dream of the easy life, a life of bright lights and big money, suddenly seemed like a nightmare. It held no interest for him. He felt no desire to be a part of it. "It was an astounding experience to have all of that come unglued before your eyes," he said.

He began to consider alternatives to living a life that now seemed empty and unattractive to him. A Catholic graduate of St. Louis University, he naturally considered the religious life. Several siblings had gone that route already. At some point, he wrote to Gethsemani's abbot, expressing interest in seeing what life was like there. He made an extended retreat during a dreary stretch of February, a time of reflection that helped him make up his mind. He applied to enter and was accepted.

He remembers vividly "the day of departure," when he said good-bye to friends and family in St. Louis, believing that from that point forward, he would see them, at most, once a year. "It was like pulling an oak tree out by its roots," he said.

Today, nearly half a century later, Brother Raphael has served his community as prior, the second-in-command to the abbot, and as head of Gethsemani Farms, the business that keeps the monastery afloat. In the 1950s he was one of the monks who helped launch the business, creating a thriving mail-order demand for the abbey's homemade food products and ensuring the community's financial security for years to come. He has traveled across the United States and in Europe in that business role. He has appeared on radio and TV, hosted dignitaries on whistle-stop tours of the abbey, and served as a spokesman when the press has come calling. Not exactly what he had in mind when he gave up the things of the world, but a role he accepts with grace and enthusiasm.

At seventy-nine, he looks back on his Miami Beach epiphany and concedes that his call to the monastic life actually began long before that night on Collins Avenue. "The longer you stay here and look back with kind of a smile, you see that there are other reasons that you've discovered were at work that you weren't perhaps all that conscious of. It's not like you turn your back on the world. It's more that I always felt there was something deeper than I was experiencing. God put books in front of me and people for me to meet, to throw light on certain things for me."

Heeding a Voice Within

Like Brother Raphael, many monks can look back and see a pattern of connections with people and places that, one by one, led him them to the monastery. God works in mysterious ways, the monks will tell you.

A native of New Jersey, Brother Joshua Brands knew little about Gethsemani when he moved to Kentucky in the 1970s. He came to study for the Catholic priesthood at St. Mary's College, a seminary that, after his graduation, was closed and converted to a prison. It's located not far from Gethsemani in a neighboring county.

Brother Joshua's first impression of his future monastic home was not altogether positive, but it planted a seed that grew into a lifetime commitment. "My first exposure to Gethsemani was my first week at St. Mary's," he said. "We came over for vespers. I thought the place looked spooky and strange."

Later, on the way to Florida for spring break, he stopped by one of Gethsemani's daughter houses near Atlanta, Holy Spirit Abbey in Conyers, Georgia. "I fell in love with the place, the whole idea, the romance. That was God's first hook in me," he recalled.

In 1989, after abandoning his studies for the priesthood and working for a time in his family's jewelry business in New Jersey, he entered Gethsemani. Five years later, at the age of forty-three, he made his solemn profession as a Trappist. "God would not let me rest until I did something about looking into the monastic life," said Brother Joshua. "It, the call, was always there no matter how or what I did. It wouldn't leave me alone until I answered in some way."

Oddly enough, for some, the call to become a monk begins with a powerful distaste for the whole idea. Brother Rene Richie, of Detroit, recalls first hearing about Trappists in seventh grade as part of a class lesson on Catholic religious life. His teacher, a nun, described monasteries in the bleakest, least-attractive terms. This was, after all, the early 1940s, when life at Gethsemani was at its most austere. He recalled, "She went through the whole thing. They don't eat meat. They don't listen to radio. They don't read newspapers. They don't read comic books. I said, 'Well that's not for me.' I remember that. It impressed me very much, that life, but my answer was no. I remember I went home and told my parents that there was a monastery where they didn't do any of those things. And I said, 'That's not for me.'"

No matter how negative Brother Rene's initial reaction to the Trappist regimen may have been, that first strong impression lingered. Later, as a teenager, he dated a young woman steadily for two years; but in spite of the relationship, he felt oddly unhappy and at loose ends. Not long after he and his girlfriend broke up, he heard about a historical novel by Father Raymond Flanagan, a Gethsemani monk who wrote fictional stories based on real-life events. The novel was *The Man Who Got Even with God,* one of Father Raymond's most popular books. It told the story of Gethsemani's first American-born monk. Shortly after hearing of the book, Brother Rene spotted a copy of Thomas Merton's *Seven Storey Mountain* in a doctor's office as he was waiting to be called by the receptionist. He felt that, through these two authors, he was being urged to get to know Gethsemani. It seemed like more than coincidence.

So he read both books, became intrigued, and made a retreat at Gethsemani. A few months later, in 1950, at the age of twenty-two, he decided he wanted to enter the community—if they would have him. His mother was fairly typical in her reaction to the news: she was not happy about it. His father, on the other hand, supported his decision. Later, when his parents made separate visits to Gethsemani, his mother's response to the monastery was, "It looks like a prison." His father disagreed with her. "No," he said, "it looks like a big farm."

Brother Rene attributes his parents' very different reactions to the fact that, unlike his father, his mother was allowed to see the monastery only from the outside. Women visitors were still restricted to the public areas of the monastery in those days. Brother Rene remembers eating meals with her in the family guesthouse, a small hotel on the hill across the highway from the monastery. When bells rang, he had to hurry back to church alone. His father, on the other hand, was able to stay on the monastery side of the road, attend services, and observe the comings and goings of the monks.

Brother Rene said that separating from his parents was not a major trauma. Today, at seventy-two, he describes himself as a "pragmatist," the kind of person who doesn't notice what's missing but focuses instead on what is present.

Ideal versus Reality

The week Brother Rene entered Gethsemani, Brother Luke Armour was born in New York City. Like Brother Rene, Brother Luke was twenty-two when he made his decision to become a monk, and he too had read Merton's *Seven Storey Mountain* at an impressionable age. Brother Luke didn't like the book, however. Years later, he reread it and found it more agreeable, but at the first reading he found it uninspiring.

It is said that half of all retreatants and half of all men who enter Gethsemani first heard about the monastery by reading Merton's books. To Brother Luke, the former guestmaster, that's a blessing and a curse. Some of Merton's earlier books led many of his readers—including some who became monks—to adopt a romanticized notion of Trappist life. When confronted with the hard realities of living in community, they grew disappointed, frustrated, and in some cases angry. Much has changed in the church since Merton's death in 1968, and the monastery is a far different place today.

Sometimes the tension between the idealized image of monastic life that a novice brings with him and the hard reality of day-to-day monasticism becomes overwhelming, and the novice opts to leave. Sometimes other factors contribute to a monk's departure. Whatever the reasons for a monk's leaving, it is never taken lightly by the community. There was a time, before the reforms of the 1960s, when a defection from the community was greeted as a failure on the monk's part. Today a departure is more apt to be handled with compassion and emotional support. Ties are maintained. Former monks are invited back for special occasions. Some regularly attend Mass at the abbey and make frequent retreats.

In an effort to reduce their losses, Trappist communities began tightening up their admission procedures in the 1970s in the wake of the great exodus of men and women from Catholic religious orders. More attention was focused on the selection process itself.

One major change was that monasteries began to discourage younger applicants. Experience showed that younger monks were greater risks because they had not had time to live independently before leaping into community life.

Brother Elias Dietz was one of those younger men whose admission was delayed because of his age. He remembers first becoming interested in the Trappists as a teenager, while studying to be a priest. He made a retreat at Gethsemani at that time and expressed interest in switching from the seminary to the monastery. Gethsemani asked him to delay his decision, however, to give it more thought while he continued his seminary studies. Although he was unhappy about being turned away, he did what they asked, and waited. "My attraction was very strong, over a long period," he said. "And I was tired of being given a hard time."

In 1988, a decade after he first expressed interest, Brother Elias was given the go-ahead to join the Gethsemani community. But then, at the age of twenty-eight, he faced resistance on another front: his parents. Although he had discussed with them his desire to be a monk many times over the years, they were taken aback emotionally by the news. "Towards the end, you know, they were hanging on, asking, 'Are you sure you want to do this?' You feel a certain amount of guilt," he said. In time, however, his parents came to accept that the decision was the right one. "They see that I'm happy here," he said.

Today, several years after our conversation about his call to Gethsemani, Brother Elias lives in Rome, where he now serves the Cistercian order as secretary to the abbot general, Dom Bernardo Olivera.

Life after the Monastery

For some men, the path that leads to a monastic life is circular. After years of preparing to become a monk, or even after taking final vows, they end up back in the secular world. Many who leave, like Michael Brown of Cistercian Lay Contemplatives, find ways to apply monastic principles and ideals to the larger community outside the cloister. In doing so, the meaning of their call grows richer.

But no matter how things turn out down the road, a departure from the monastic life is hard on the individual who leaves as well as the community that is left. It usually stirs up questions in the monks who remain, sometimes strengthening their own vocations, sometimes creating bouts of doubt.

Brother Jonah McCarty left Gethsemani in 1999, after six years of work and study intended to lead to his solemn profession. Several years before his departure, Hugh McCarty, as he is now known again, talked to me at length about his personal experience of monastic life.

He was candid about the day-to-day challenges and, even then, keenly aware of the possibility that he might not reach his goal. "The hardest thing here is just living with yourself day in and day out. There are no distractions, really. It's very difficult," he said. "I've never been bored. But lonely? Yes. It can be lonely and extremely frustrating and, I suspect, immensely rich and rewarding—probably beyond my wildest dreams—if I can persevere, which I have doubts about."

Referring to his late-life call, Brother Jonah likened his journey to that of "the Jews who wandered in the desert for forty years." He entered Gethsemani at the age of forty, after a good bit of roaming on his own. Like Brother Joshua, he attended St. Mary's College for a few years, then decided the priesthood was not the right path and served a five-year stint in the navy. He had grown up, one of twelve children, on a farm in Owensboro, Kentucky, and he liked working outdoors. So after his navy stint, he held a series of construction jobs.

Growing up in Owensboro, an Ohio River town one hundred miles west of Gethsemani, he didn't hear much about the monastery. At St. Mary's, however, he met a monk who told him about the life there.

Brother Jonah was fascinated by what he heard and wondered if this might be the path for him. But he resisted thinking too much about it, telling himself, "I've got places to go and things to do."

Nevertheless, for twenty years the notion simmered on a back burner, where the flame never died out. For five years before entering Gethsemani in 1993, Brother Jonah grew increasingly sure this was the life for him. "I had said, 'No, no, no, no.' And finally one day I said, 'Okay.' It was just kind of a leap in the dark."

The first two years at Gethsemani were a rollercoaster ride for Brother Jonah. He described them as the best years of his life and also a disquieting time when he "cried more tears than in the previous twenty years."

The monastery felt like home, he said, but a home he wasn't sure he might not run away from at some point. He described his novice years as an unsettled period. He expressed gratitude for the personal freedom and spiritual guidance he received, especially from Brother Gerlac O'Loughlin, the novicemaster at Gethsemani for more than two decades. But he also talked about how overwhelmed he sometimes felt, how hard it was to take on so much personal responsibility for his spiritual life. "Brother Gerlac advises me and comes up with suggestions and recommendations," Brother Jonah said. "He never says, 'Do this or don't do that.'" He recognized that this was a "more mature way of dealing with life," but he felt uncertain and confused when faced with so much freedom.

That statement reminded me of something I was told a decade earlier by a thirty-eight-year-old Canadian monk who was, at the time, a few years away from taking his solemn vows. Brother Benjamin had said, "Nothing is expected of you except 'to be.' That sounds great until you have to do it." Not long after we had that conversation, he too left Gethsemani.

Brother Benjamin had said something else about the difficulty of making the transition from outsider to monk that I had written down in my notebook. It was an insight that reached to the heart of what Catholics sometimes call the "vocation problem" in the U.S. today. "Faith is very important, and trust, and the willingness to be part of a community and to let others help us—and not to be so individualistic and independent, as North Americans always want to be," Brother Benjamin said.

Individualism—the belief in the separate and autonomous self—has become so basic to the collective American psyche that it is hard for some men who've grown up in the culture to make the transition to living communally, as monks must learn to do.

On the other hand, many of the older monks at Gethsemani are World War II veterans. Several served in the Marine Corps. They learned to work together in military service, to cooperate toward a common aim, and they've carried that ensemble-player attitude over to community life. There is a book commemorating the hundredth anniversary of the founding of Gethsemani that includes a note from its abbot, Father James Fox, in which he uses the most vigorous patriotic military jargon to celebrate the spiritual efforts of his then-youthful community.

Times have changed at Gethsemani, as they have everywhere. The community is no longer youthful. Of its sixty-five monks, about fifteen live in the infirmary, which serves as an on-site nursing home for the senior brothers. Today's novice is unlikely to have fought in a war or to have served in any sort of military service. For that matter, he may not have experienced much teamwork at all, other than perhaps on an athletic field.

Other changes within monasteries, beneficial in themselves, exacerbate the problem, according to Father Felix, the former guestmaster at Gethsemani. The monk today has greater personal autonomy in regard to his spiritual life. The old days of an abbot or spiritual director dictating a man's prayer life or monitoring his reading material are long gone, for example. "You have lots more choices today," Father Felix said. "You have more freedom. You can read novels and classic literature all the time and neglect other areas of our tradition, like reading from Scripture. You could listen to music or you could pick up hobbies, anything from gardening to hiking."

Father Felix said there is a difference, however, between having this kind of freedom in a monastery and having it the secular world. In a monastery each monk presumably has a one-on-one relationship with a personal guide or mentor, known as a spiritual director. This is another monk whose duty is to step in and nudge a brother when his behaviors or attitudes become counterproductive or destructive. The two monks meet regularly so that trust builds and understanding grows. Spiritual direction is one of the aspects of monastic life that has begun to grow popular in the lay Catholic world too, as more and more people receive professional training in this kind of counseling. The process is sometimes described as spiritual therapy, and it requires a similar kind of trusting relationship to work. "It really doesn't work for a person who doesn't have that kind of relationship with another person to go up to him and just straighten him out," Father Felix said.

Formation is the training process by which a man becomes a monk, a full-fledged member of a monastic community. It's a conversion process that helps him let go of habits and mindsets that no longer apply and prepares him for a way of life that has its own distinct rhythms, rules, and rubrics. Novices usually meet with their novice master several times a week as a group and individually.

Another integral part of the process of becoming a monk is accepting the monastic view of work. "When they live by the labor of their hands, then they are really monks," St. Benedict says in the Rule. In an aging community, like that of Gethsemani, younger monks often are called upon to do their assigned jobs (making cheese, say, or preparing foods in the kitchen), as well as take up the slack on jobs assigned

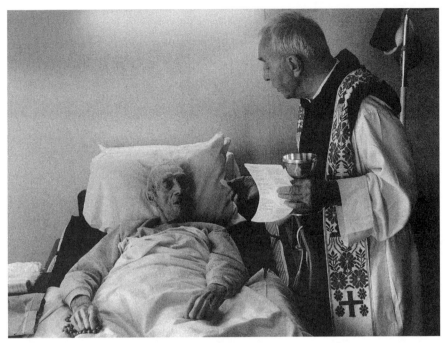

Bringing Communion to an elderly brother in the monastery infirmary.

to their elder brothers who may not be as efficient as they were in their younger days. Taking responsibility for the work that keeps the community afloat is part of what a monk-in-training has to learn to do.

In 1995, when I talked to Brother Jonah about the work assigned to the five novices in his class, he shook his head and laughed. "Whoever needs help hollers for us. The rest of the community must think there are fifteen of us, because they're always wanting a little bit more than we can give."

When the going got rough and he began to doubt his vocation and wonder if the monastery was where he belonged, Brother Jonah—a farm boy at heart—found encouragement and comfort in the hills and woods surrounding Gethsemani. "A bunch of men living together in a community have a tendency to have a lot of sharp edges and a lot of rough spots," he said. "We have moments when we need something to be gentle and to calm us, and what better than the hills and the knobs as God made them? We can go out and relax and let our guard down. Go out on the porch, so to speak, and watch."

At the time, Brother Jonah's comments sounded like the ruminations of anyone who is trying to achieve a hard-to-reach goal. In retrospect, they sound like a foreshadowing of what was to come in his personal journey. Today, Hugh McCarty is pursuing a master's degree in social work at a Catholic university in Louisville. He works part-time at night to help foot the bills. He isn't sure what he will do with his advanced degree, but he is considering working with prison inmates as "a special ministry."

Testing the Call

How can a man or, for that matter, a novicemaster know when a calling is strong enough to withstand the emotional and physical rigors of monastic life? What is the test? Who scores it? How do you know if you're passing or failing?

In some cases, you just know. Father Damien, the abbot of Gethsemani, remembers suddenly being aware one day near the end of his training that something had changed for him. He said, "I just knew I was a monk then. It wasn't as if somebody said something to me. There is just a point at which a relationship forms. Two become one. And you don't have to be told."

Father Damien compared it, as others have, to the spiritual bond that takes place between two people that then leads them to the formal relationship of marriage.

But before that point, when a man is simply inquiring about entering, what are the standards that a community of monks must apply to individuals?

A brochure in the lobby of the Gethsemani guesthouse talks about

A monk in traditional Trappist habit (clothing). The official garb of a Trappist monk includes a white tunic; a black scapular, or hooded apron; and a leather belt. A white hooded cowl, or cloak, is also worn at certain times of day and on special occasions.

the call to monastic life as "a desire [that] needs to be tested thoroughly." The brochure poses a series of questions that a monastery must ask of those who apply for entry as well as those already in training. They include the following:

How well is the applicant using the means to holiness and prayer available in his present situation? Does he have the capacity for healthy relationships? Can he spend time in holy reading and solitary prayer? Is he willing to work at whatever is assigned to him and does he find satisfaction in it? Does he really believe this would be a worthwhile way to spend his life?

A monastery's vocation director works closely with applicants, or "candidates," as they are sometimes called, to help them answer these questions honestly before entering the community. In contrast to the days when Brother Rene came to Gethsemani, the process of "discernment," as it is called, now takes at least a year and usually includes several extended retreats.

Once accepted into the community, the candidate becomes a postulant. For six months he shares in the work and prayers of the community while continuing to wear street clothes rather than a monk's habit. At the end of the six months he is given a new name, his hair is shaved, and he takes on the all-white novice habit. He also begins his novitiate studies, which last for two years.

The next step for a novice is to make a temporary, one-year vow, and to begin wearing the black Trappist apron, called a "scapular," and the traditional leather belt. He must renew his temporary vow annually for at least three years before taking his solemn, perpetual vows—the lifetime commitment to the Trappist way of life that is celebrated at a special Mass.

This discernment period leading up to final vows, when both the community and the individual are deciding whether they are in both their best interests, can last no longer than nine years. To delay one's solemn profession longer than that is, essentially, a decision to leave the monastery. Some monks opt to become priests as well, but that is a separate process, requiring additional education.

As novicemaster, Brother Gerlac is responsible for the spiritual development of his monks-in-training. In that role he keeps an eye out for behaviors and characteristics that help or hinder adjustment to monastic life. "Some people come to work out problems or to avoid them. But you can't forget your problems here. Some people try too hard to work them out through prayer," Brother Gerlac told me. He used the example of the troubled young woman in J. D. Salinger's *Franny and Zooey* who thinks she can escape the problems in her life by incessantly chanting the Jesus Prayer. "Though it's not as hard as it was, it's still a hard life. But it's a healthy life for a healthy person," Brother Gerlac said.

Every effort is made to make sure candidates are healthy in a psychological, emotional sense. A battery of tests is administered to prospective monks, and personal interviews are conducted. Age limits are imposed: those under twenty-two or over forty-five are usually considered bad risks for adapting to the restrictions of monastic vows.

The new name a novice is given serves as a reminder of his break with the outside world as well as a celebration of his new identity as a member of the community. Most monks are given the names of Cistercian leaders or saints. Hence, Gethsemani's rosters over the years have been filled with names that sound exotic to modern ears—names such as Nivard, Bede, Chrysogonus, Hilarion, Aelred, and Gerlac.

Brother Gerlac, a man with a dry sense of humor and a ready smile, once told me the story of how he got his name. It seems the abbot was away visiting another monastery when it came time for naming the novices. In his absence, another monk did the honors. Not everybody was pleased with this monk's choices, Gerlac recalled, and one novice decided to take matters into his own hands. He waited until the abbot returned and then requested a new name. "The abbot said fine, and renamed him Sylvester. I decided to stick with Gerlac."

Gethsemani seeks men, like Gerlac, with a sense of humor, men whose self-esteem is solid, and whose ability to accept limits on personal behavior is not in question. "You can't just go out to a ballgame or watch TV or get a drink at a pub when you want to," said Father Michael Casagram, a vocations director at Gethsemani.

Above all, the trait that the monastery values most in its monks is the ability to love, deeply and broadly. Monastic life has long been described in religious literature as a "school for charity." Father Michael said that the true monk understands love as a desire "to share your life with others and to suffer the consequences of that." Monastic life "is not a life of having mystical experiences," he said. "People tend to romanticize us, and that holds up for about three days."

I think, finally, of a remark written down among my notes from a long-ago retreat—a comment that a monk made to me when I asked him just what goes on, day to day, in a monk's life that is so extraordinary. What is it that requires so much love, understanding, and deep faith in God? The contemplative life, this monk told me, is simply this: "a good system of taking you apart and letting you see inside yourself."

After all is said and done, after the vows are sworn and the belt slung about the waist, during the good times and especially the bad times, what a monk sees when he looks inside himself is that which he has promised to never stop seeking: God.

4

Daily Work:
By the Labor of Their Hands

The Christian finds in human work a small part of the cross of Christ and accepts it in the same spirit of redemption in which Christ accepted his cross for us.

—POPE JOHN PAUL II, FROM HIS 1984 PAPAL ENCYCLICAL, *LABOREM EXERCENS* ("ON HUMAN WORK")

Duty Calls

If prayer sets the back-and-forth rhythm of the monk's day, work establishes its tempo. Mornings, after Mass is over and breakfast eaten, a Trappist monastery picks up speed. You sense a seriousness of purpose in the way the monks move. They wear their work clothes now: T-shirts and jeans, sneakers and baseball caps. The habits of white and black are put away for later use, perhaps to greet visitors at the retreat house, or for attendance at evening services. In corridors and on sidewalks, where an aura of peace and meditation had earlier pervaded, an air of industry now takes its place.

And retreatants are welcome to join the monastic work force at any time. Signs in the dining area make it clear that anyone who wishes to help out may do so. Some wipe tables after meals. Some sweep sidewalks and hallways. Some water plants. It can enhance a retreat immeasurably to take part in the rhythm of the community's workday.

On this fourth day of my Gethsemani retreat, I begin to sense a hierarchy of jobs within the monastery and to associate certain monks with certain duties. Even the most reclusive retreatant would, by now, recognize who the kitchen-detail monks are; who the chaplain is; who has the job of guestmaster, leader of the *schola* (a small choir that sings apart from the rest of the community at special times during church services), retreat-house receptionist, gardener.

The Abbey's Spiritual Father

Most recognizable is, of course, the abbot. He is the one who blesses the crowd with a sprinkling of holy water at the end of compline and is the obvious chief priest at the abbey's Sunday celebration of Mass, the central worship service of Catholics everywhere. His title, abbot, is derived from the Aramaic word *abba*, for "father," and, at least within Trappist orders, he must be an ordained priest or be prepared to train to become one upon election. (Today, sixteen of Gethsemani's sixty-five monks are priests; the others have chosen not to be ordained.)

The abbot's duties are spelled out in the Rule of St. Benedict, where they are described in terms that make it clear that the office calls for being more than simply an administrator or even a teacher. The abbot is, according to the Rule, a "spiritual father" empowered by God to command and direct his monks on their journey to union with God. A monk is expected to offer "unfeigned and humble love" to his abbot, not out of any belief in his infallibility or omniscience, but because the abbot takes the place of Christ in his community.

The Rule includes a catalog of leadership characteristics that an abbot ought to possess, including discretion, wisdom, prudence, and sensitivity to individual differences among men. And yet, St. Benedict, with his customary shrewdness and keen understanding of the ways of human relationships, also made provisions for an abbot's limitations and deficiencies. Aware of the dangers of a vow of obedience in a house with a flawed leader, the Rule specifies that an abbot must seek the counsel of his monks. Clearly, Benedict wanted to protect his monasteries from rule by autocrats or incompetents; he intrinsically trusted the collective inspired wisdom of the monastic community.

The other safeguard built into the Rule is the abbatial election process, which has evolved over time. Today, most Trappist abbots are elected by their communities for six-year terms that are renewable indefinitely. As an abbot's tenure comes to a close, he may decide to resign, opening the door to new leadership, or he may wish to stay in office and run for reelection. This decision usually comes after consultation with the abbot of the community's mother house, the monastery from which it has spun off, so to speak. At Gethsemani, that would be the abbot of the Abbey of Melleray in France. In like manner, an abbatial election at the Abbey of the Holy Spirit in Conyers, Georgia, would come after consultation with the abbot of Gethsemani, the head of its mother house.

With six daughter houses to look after, Gethsemani's abbot travels a lot, by necessity. The first month of his tenure as Gethsemani's abbot, Father Damien flew to Utah to oversee a change of administration at the Abbey of the Holy Trinity near Salt Lake City. Father Timothy Kelly, his predecessor, remembers how swiftly the baton was passed to him when he was elected abbot in 1973, at the age of thirty-seven. "The day before I was elected," Father Timothy said, "I could tell the farm boss something and he'd laugh in my face. The day after I was elected, I was suddenly an expert on raising cows, selling cheese, the mystical life, caring for aging people in an infirmary." He smiled. "That's not quite so."

At present, Gethsemani's abbot can count on visiting its six daughter houses every couple of years to evaluate the abbots there. Three times during his term of office, Father Timothy decided it was time for an abbot to resign, perhaps against his wishes. "I was getting a reputation," he said, with a smile. "Watch your scalp—here he comes."

There is a saying among Trappists that the community tends to elect the kind of abbot it needs to lead it to the next stage, even when it isn't clear yet what that next stage will be. Father Timothy, a Canadian, was abbot for nearly three decades. He ushered in changes that no one could have imagined possible at the time of his election: the welcoming of women to the retreat house; permission to visitors at Mass to sit in areas of the church formerly reserved for monks; a major overhaul of the guesthouse; the sale of the abbey's last herds of blue-ribbon milking cows and beef cattle; visits from Asian monastic leaders, including a retreat of several days by the Dalai Lama, the exiled spiritual leader of Tibet.

Brother Paul Quenon, a monk of Gethsemani since the age of eighteen, said Father Timothy also transformed the role the abbot played in terms of community work. Before he took charge, Gethsemani's abbots tended to detach themselves from the mundane jobs of monastic life. They stayed in their offices and developed what Brother Paul calls a "monarchical" or "aristocratic" style.

But Father Timothy, right up to the last day of his tenure, did any job that needed doing—and still does. "He works in the refectory," Brother Paul said. "He takes his turn serving tables. He runs the tractor—at least he did when we had a farm. He's got more of a democratic style."

Abbots are not always elected from strictly within their communities, although at Gethsemani all but one has been an insider. Daughter houses may elect an abbot from within the ranks of their mother house, for example. This has led to the loss of a number of Gethsemani's monks over the years. Father Felix Donahue, the former retreat-house chaplain, was plucked by the Trappists at Novo Mundo in Brazil. Father Flavian Burns, Gethsemani's abbot at the time of Merton's death in 1968, was later elected to lead the Trappist monastery at Berryville, Virginia. Father

Francis Kline, a musician trained at the Julliard School of Music, left Gethsemani to become abbot of Mepkin Abbey in South Carolina. Father John Eudes Bamberger left when elected abbot of Abbey of the Genesee in New York.

A Gethsemani monk who is elected a superior elsewhere always has the right to return to his home community, where he has taken his vow of stability. Some do, some don't.

One of the subtle checks and balances of Trappist life is the policy that prohibits an abbot from serving as confessor to any of his monks. This is a safeguard, designed to protect monks from revealing their spiritual vulnerabilities to the man who is, after all, responsible for assigning work and making administrative recommendations that greatly affect the individual monk's life within the community. "The brothers should approach the abbot with confidence and be able to reveal to him freely and spontaneously the thoughts arising in their hearts," the Constitutions of the Cistercian Order specify. "Nevertheless, the abbot should in no way induce them to manifest their consciences to him."

At Trappist monasteries, as at most Benedictine houses today, major decisions are usually made by committee, through a process of discussion and discernment within the Abbot's council. The council is made up of other monks who hold significant leadership positions within the community. The treasurer and head of the food-production department, for example, are standing members of the council. The other group that assists the abbot is the business committee. Big issues are generally settled by majority vote of the entire house after hearing recommendations from these groups.

Running a Monastery, Day to Day

What are the other important positions in a monastery like Gethsemani? The prior is second-in-command, the monk who takes over when the abbot is away. In the abbot's absence he bestows the compline blessing and gives "chapter talks," the regular homilies ordinarily delivered to the community by the abbot on Sunday mornings after lauds. He also presides at other chapter meetings in the abbot's absence, such as the weekly Thursday evening "town hall" gatherings.

In earlier days, when monasteries were truly self-sufficient organizations, the "cellarer"—the monk in charge of provisions—was a powerful job to hold within Trappist communities. Today, at Gethsemani, the title refers to the monk in charge of maintaining the physical plant at his monastery as well as providing for the care and feeding of his fellow monks. If a roof needs repair, he oversees the crew that fixes it. He sees to it that the larders are stocked with ingredients so the kitchen cook can prepare the meals. If the church needs renovation, it falls to him to be a kind of general contractor.

In the 1940s and 1950s, when Gethsemani was bursting with men who arrived in the wake of Merton's best-selling autobiography, the cellarer's job was a massive one. John Dorsey, a civil engineer, held the post until 1969, when he left the Trappist order and moved to nearby Louisville. Dorsey traveled widely, he said, scouting land that might be suitable for future daughter houses.

Called a "foundation," a new house involves more than simply securing property for it. It requires that a monastery have monks to spare—"founders" to send to the site, to set up a new community, and to run it. From 1944 to 1955 Gethsemani established five new monasteries, in Georgia, Utah, New York, South Carolina, and California. In 1966 the community took over an existing monastery in Santiago, Chile, the Monastery of Miraflores. Dorsey (known then as Brother Clement) was the monk who explored the potential locations, investigating the pros and cons of various sites. "About a third of the time, I was someplace other than the monastery," Dorsey recalled.

But those trips were only a part of the major role the cellarer played

Chapter meetings are held on Sundays after lauds, and on Thursday evenings before compline. Here, Abbot Damien Thompson leads a discussion.

at the time. Dorsey recalls massive construction projects that he supervised, all of which were prompted by the need to accommodate the growing number of men who were knocking at Gethsemani's doors at midcentury. In the Trappist tradition, most of the work was done by the monks themselves. They excavated beneath the monastery buildings to create a network of basement rooms. They erected a 160-foot water tower with a thirty-thousand-gallon holding tank. They created a "monkmade" lake to feed the water system. They added a wing on the monastery to house novices. They built a fireproof horse barn.

Dorsey's favorite maxim about monastic life, which came out of his experience during those years, is a simple and straightforward, if humorous, take on the two most important things a monk should keep in mind: "To do as you're told and to do as you're told."

On his last exploratory trip, he remembers leaving the monastery, headed for California on his own, on a summer day when his brothers—including his abbot—were in the fields working. "It was humorous. I was in my black traveling suit with my suitcase going out the gate, and the abbot was out in the sweet potato patch, hoeing—where I should have been, I thought."

Father Felix also has a comical image burned into his memory from that era: a parade of eager young monks lined up, tools in hand, sent out in silence to work at jobs they were not always qualified to perform. "Some days we would all have a common work project," he recalled. "Usually it was cutting down firewood out in the woods. You'd have a line of two hundred people heading out for work, dropping trees on each other. A bunch of city kids with axes, a menace to each other."

Those days are over. Few major construction jobs are called for these days; there is no need to expand. The average size of a Trappist monastery today—twenty-five nuns or monks—is less than half what it was in former times.

Today, one of the primary duties of Gethsemani's cellarer is to oversee the growing lay workforce: that is, the employees from outside the monastery who are hired for specific jobs. The number of lay workers has increased significantly over the past fifty years, as the average age of the community has crept upward and the mail-order business skyrocketed.

In 1952, for example, in the days when Dorsey was scouting land for daughter houses, Gethsemani hired virtually no lay workers. Today, 12 percent of the budget goes for salaries to non-Trappist employees. Lay men and women, mostly residents of neighboring small towns, perform a variety of work at Gethsemani, ranging from carpentry and construction jobs to retreat-house kitchen duties and clerical tasks related to mail-order sales.

Like all monasteries, Gethsemani has changed dramatically. The roster of the first forty-four monks who came from France to set up the first Trappist monastery at Gethsemani still exists. Written in 1848, it lists the occupations of the men and testifies to the diverse talents among them: a mason, a nailsmith, a carder, a tinsmith, a cabinet maker, a miller, a weaver, a barber, two stone cutters, a painter, a harness maker, a bookbinder, a mechanic, three blacksmiths, a woodworker, a bee-keeper, a turner, two carpenters, two bakers, a sculptor, and a physician. They clearly needed to hire few outsiders to round out their expertise, as today's monasteries must do.

Who knows how they (or St. Benedict, for that matter) would respond to such a major shift in monastic life? Manual labor, self-sufficiency, and communal living were the governing principles of the monastic society Benedict created. He based his Rule on a balance of prayer and work, in contrast to the merely meditative seclusion that was the hallmark of earlier forms of monasticism in both East and West.

Again, this was in some ways a countercultural concept. Manual labor was not highly valued in Roman and Greek times, in part because both societies had relied on slave labor to get their work done. Jews, on the other hand, had a tradition of alternating work and rest in the pattern of their lives, and they had promoted a belief in the value of discipline and communal security as well as a disdain for idleness and lack of industry. So, the monastic principle of manual work flowed out of the Judeo-Christian tradition at the same time that it challenged the conventions of Roman and Greek society.

Today, as then, monks view manual labor as an opportunity to share in the divine work of creation. The work varies, naturally, from monastery to monastery. At Dubuque, Iowa, the Trappistine nuns make creamy caramel candy. At Gethsemani's daughter house in Utah the monks sell honey. At Mepkin Abbey they make compost "tea," a garden fertilizer. At Vina, California, they tend their orchards, supplying prunes and walnuts to companies like Sunsweet and Diamond Walnut.

But, at its deepest level, the work of these contemplative men and women connects them in a spiritual sense to other workers around the world. It promotes a sense of altruism and selfless concern for others.

It provides a livelihood for the community and a surplus to be shared, ideally, with the poor.

Stewards of the Land

True enough, Gethsemani has no crops or animals to tend today. But several of its monks have shown a personal interest in continuing the Cistercian tradition of horticulture by maintaining gardens and nursery plots on the grounds. Visitors to Gethsemani often enjoy the creative handiwork of Brother Harold Thibodeau, who can be seen puttering in the flower gardens, herb plots, and ponds near the retreat house and just inside the monastic enclosure. He is always eager to introduce a retreatant to his plantings.

Although St. Benedict could not have realized it, his philosophy of work—and his insistence on building monasteries in fertile, fruitful regions—led to the development of model farming techniques and systems throughout medieval Europe. It generated centers of trade and industry. As monasteries grew into thriving compounds, St. Benedict's work ethic produced a growing number of jobs for skilled craftsmen and artisans who hailed from the village and towns that grew up nearby.

The Trappist monk is a type of Cistercian monk, which is itself a type of Benedictine monk. The Cistercians were a reform branch of the Benedictines—an outgrowth of a rebel group that left its home monastery at Molesmes, France, in 1098, under the leadership of the abbot Robert, to set up a community of its own based on a stricter interpretation of the Rule. These Cistercian monks later were reformed again, in the seventeenth century, by a group later called Trappists, after the Abbey of La Trappe, the place where their strict regime was carried out.

In both instances the reforms were an effort to return to a more ascetic way of life, which included laboring longer and more rigorously at their jobs. But the reformers' emphasis on hard work was not some attempt at holier-than-thou, conspicuous piety. The Cistercian insistence on manual labor, some historians say, was a powerful political statement—a protest against the inordinate wealth that many of the feudal abbeys of the era had obtained. "The Cistercians could not accept the notion of a life of contemplation in which the interior peace and leisure of the contemplative were luxuries purchased by the exploitation of serfs and the taxation of the poor," Merton wrote in his history of the order. "St. Benedict had prescribed that the monk was to be the poorest of the poor and live by his own labor."

Certainly the monks of the Middle Ages had their work cut out for them. In his 1995 best-seller, *How the Irish Saved Civilization*, Thomas Cahill explores the pivotal part that Christian monks played in preserving Western culture during the chaotic fifth century. In those dire days Irish monks steadfastly and fastidiously copied every piece of literature they could find, reproducing manuscripts regardless of their authorship. Determined to save civilization in the only way they knew how, they copied the works of pagans and Christians alike, in Greek and in Latin, and in so doing, triggered a revival of literacy at a time when Europe was under siege by barbarians.

Today, a monk's work is not so exalted in purpose, nor so mammoth in scope. In fact, work for the Trappist monk is now, as it has always been, more a matter of balance and humility than glory or grandeur. Work is as basic and essential to the monastic way of life as prayer and reading are.

Rather than saving an entire civilization by the work of his hands, the modern monk is likely to have more practical purposes in mind as he goes about his daily business—baking fruitcakes, wrapping cheese, sending out mail-order invoices. He is apt to be working to keep his community afloat financially rather than attempting to rescue civilization from the jaws of savages. He is likely to be working to create funds beyond those needed to maintain the abbey and to support the community—funds to be shared with the needy as close as the isolated Appalachian settlements of eastern Kentucky or as far-flung as the teeming streets of Calcutta, India.

Today at Gethsemani, work is the monk's link to the larger global village.

Making a Livelihood

In 1951 Dom James Fox, no doubt drawing on his Harvard Business School education, decided to set up a business arm of the monastery. Called Gethsemani Farms, its purpose was to produce, package, and market the abbey's growing line of food products. The monks had for a long time baked bread and made cheese, which they sold locally. Soon, a new product—homemade fruitcake—became available as well.

Today, Gethsemani Farms is what keeps the monastery afloat. Its products are sold by mail order, phone bank, and Internet. The monks also have a website (www.monks.org), where products can be purchased online. In 1952, a year after the business was started, its profits accounted for 8 percent of the abbey's sources of support. Today, it accounts for 60 percent. The next largest source of revenue, at 16 percent, is the continuing royalties accrued from the works of its published authors.

Yet, depending on the season, the business sometimes accounts for close to 100 percent of the activity at the monastery. A retreatant isn't likely to notice, but six days a week throughout the year, except for a brief hiatus before Christmas, monks make cheese, fruitcake, and Kentucky bourbon fudge by hand in various buildings inside the enclosure.

The hands-down busiest time of year for marketing and sales is, of course, the period from fall through Christmas. Most products bought at that time are shipped out as gifts. By the last week of the big rush nearly every monk who can work is involved in some aspect of the order taking or shipping of food products. In addition, lay workers are hired as needed. And of course, nothing else at the monastery stops or even slows down when the food business cranks up. There are still retreatants and monks to feed, clothes to be washed, holiday liturgies to be planned, and buildings to be maintained.

In recent years, enthusiastic reviews by food writers in publications as prestigious as the *Wall Street Journal* have created huge demand for Gethsemani Farms products. One recent holiday season, the monks ran out of fruitcake before all the orders were filled. The website had to be shut down. The following year, production was increased, and there was no problem supplying customers. However, it meant that the community was stretched to its limit, and even more lay workers had to be hired.

Such work is tedious, and hardly the stuff of spiritual rapture: typing, manning telephone banks, deciphering handwritten mail orders, shrink-wrapping boxes, applying shipping labels, running forklifts, dealing with truckdrivers. But it is the work that maintains the monastery, just as milking cows and baling hay did in the old days.

Sometimes the mindlessness or the technology of the mail-order food business makes a monk wonder about the work he is doing. I once listened to a young monk talk about his own struggle to come to terms with the discrepancy between an admittedly romantic view of harvesting corn on a monastic farm and the reality of reaping fudge orders from a website. He said he resisted his particular assignment, a highly technical computer-related job. He was unable to find the meaning in it, the connection to the life of his brothers and the goals of simplicity and poverty that he was pursuing when he entered Gethsemani. His struggle ultimately led him to a belief that "being simple and poor" means "doing what needs to be done." Sometimes that is hitching yourself to a keyboard, filling orders for fruitcake and pesto cheese rather than toiling in the fields of God's creation.

Putting God to Work in the Business Department

At the age of seventy-nine, Brother Raphael has spent more than half his life helping to run the business that keeps the monastery going. He was assigned to the fledgling operation in 1957 and remembers thinking at the time that "the business side" couldn't possibly be right for him. He had, after all, left that world behind when he entered Gethsemani. But he did as he was told, and today he says he sees "the providence of God in it." The job drew on his organizational skills and fulfilled a serious need within the community.

When Brother Raphael began working in the old converted barn where the business is still located, he joined Brother Frederic Collins, a monk about his age who had entered the monastery the same month he did. Brother Frederic had earned a business administration degree from the University of Kansas and had worked in Kansas City, Missouri, for the Prudential Life Insurance Company and for the Ford Motor Company. Both monks were veterans of World War II, both a bit uncertain of their new work assignments. "I was into poverty, simplicity of life," said Brother Frederic, "so it was ironic that I was made manager of a department making all that money, and was responsible for expanding it from nothing to the business it is today."

Gethsemani, like other monasteries, was in a state of flux in those years. In the longstanding tradition of Benedictine and Trappist abbeys, the community had depended on farming for its livelihood. But small farms were already headed for the endangered-species list in America, and soon religious orders themselves would be joining them there. Gethsemani needed an alternative method of supporting its compound of buildings, its acres of land, and the hundreds of men occupying them.

Apparently, the idea of finding a "business" to replace farming as a source of support came originally from George Skakel, a wealthy Connecticut friend of then-abbot Dom James Fox. The Skakel family was,

The monastery's "shops building," as it is called by the monks, houses carpentry and other workshops. It is one of Gethsemani's oldest buildings.

and continues to be, one of the abbey's benefactors, helping to support many projects, including the renovation of the retreat house in the 1980s.

The story goes that after George Skakel took a tour of the farm, he bluntly told the abbot that the monks would never be able to support themselves on such a poor "pile of rocks." Whether the story is true or apocryphal, a food-products business was launched. The monks started with cheese, improvising on the Port du Salut recipe that originated at the Trappist Abbey of Port du Salut in France. Later, they branched out to fruitcake spiked with aged Kentucky bourbon, and most recently have added bourbon fudge to the mix.

Merton, in his published journals, often railed against Gethsemani's food "industry," reflecting the views of some of his brothers at the time. He argued that it was out of character with the agrarian traditions of Trappist life.

Brother Frederic, who was drawn to Gethsemani by Merton's works, simply says, "I had a difference of opinion with him." But Frederic admits that he, too, kept feeling the pull to a simpler kind of monastic work, something that would bring him in closer relationship to the poor and the needy. Like Merton, he felt twinges of guilt when he surveyed the huge land holdings of Gethsemani, knowing that there were people without a square foot to call their own. In 1966 he joined a group of his brothers and headed for Santiago, Chile, to help out at the monastery that the community had just taken over. To his surprise, the situation he found there was not so different from back in Kentucky. "Lo and behold, I found out that the monastery had a bigger piece of property than we had here. Proportionately, they had really nice buildings. They were really affluent Americans in a poor country," he said. "Besides, I was already in my forties, and wasn't learning Spanish that well, so I decided to come back to Gethsemani."

After three years, he returned home. But he kept exploring other kinds of monastic work and lifestyles. He considered moving to one of the experimental hermitage colonies that were sprouting up in Trappist communities around the world. In 1970 his exploration ended, however. He was assigned to the post of treasurer at Gethsemani on a temporary basis, while he sorted out his future.

His temporary job turned into a lifetime's work. He's still treasurer today. "You could say Providence called me back to the treasurer's office," he laughs. While in that post, however, he's done what lots of twenty-first-century monks end up doing: holding down several jobs at one time. He has served as retreat master and vocations director, but always, "When it was time to make out the financial report for the year, I did that, too."

He finds irony in the fact that it was his "office job" that ultimately allowed him to cultivate that relationship to the poor and vulnerable that was so important to him in his younger days. "Because we have been successful here in earning enough money to support ourselves—

and that's one of the principles of this monastery—we make enough extra and receive enough donations and money from various other places that it allows us to have a very generous budget for helping the poor," Brother Frederic said.

Today, Gethsemani's charitable contributions account for 22 percent of its expenditures; in 1952 they accounted for 8 percent.

Brother Frederic helped organize a Habitat for Humanity in his neck of the Kentucky woods and served on its board as treasurer. He has also served as the abbey's liaison with various housing and welfare agencies, providing needed funds for projects on behalf of local residents.

Not by Bread Alone

The bakery opens shortly after 7:30 AM each morning, right after terce (from the Latin *tertia hora*, meaning "third hour"), the ten-minute liturgical hour that follows Mass. Monks like Brother Simeon Malone, with years of experience at fruitcake baking, begin the process. Each batch of batter is a day's work, resulting in about 275 cakes. I remember my first visit to the fruitcake bakery and the two overriding sensations I encountered as I entered the room. First there was the nearly overwhelming aroma, sweet and luscious—a heady blend of bourbon whisky, butter, fruits, and nuts. The second sensation? Silence—complete, utter quiet. Despite the work that was about to begin in that cavernous kitchen, there was no chatter, no clatter.

On one side of the room where the cakes are made sits an odd-looking contraption, a homemade machine that injects shots of bourbon into each cooled cake. Designed by one of the monks, it quickly and efficiently suffuses the cakes with about thirteen cubic centimeters of bourbon per pound of cake.

The fruitcake ingredients are prepared at the end of each day so that the batter is ready to be mixed and poured first thing in the morning.

It slips through a huge funnel into prepared pans, which a monk then slams hard on a table to settle the batter for baking.

By 9:30 the cakes are baking on the sturdy shelves of the mammoth oven. Batches of small and large cakes are alternated, with the former baking for a good two hours, and the latter coming out after an hour and a half. The half dozen or so monks on fruitcake detail are busily going about their jobs. Some place dried cherries and nuts in a decorative pattern over the tops of the freshly baked cakes. On my first visit, I remember, one of the monks working in the bakery was eighty years old, stooped over and bent, but apparently gratified to have a contribution to make to the community. His job was to smooth the tops of the uncooked cakes with a large, flat utensil.

As the last cakes are baking, the monks clean up after themselves and then begin the process of sorting and mixing ingredients for the next day. Spices are weighed, and hunks of butter and cups of honey measured. Cherries and nuts are picked over to weed out imperfections and shells. Gethsemani uses pecans from Georgia and walnuts from California, two of the states where they have daughter houses.

The monks bake six days a week, Mondays through Saturdays. They bake on Labor Day, Thanksgiving, Fourth of July, and all holidays except Catholic holy days and "solemnities," or feast days of saints, like Bernard or Benedict, who hold a special place in the hearts of Trappists. (The feast of St. Bernard, one of the most illustrious of Cistercian monks, is usually celebrated at Gethsemani with a dinner of pizza and beer, according to Brother Raphael.) The baking season is a long one, lasting from the first week of January through the first week of December.

One day out of six is reserved for baking bread—white and whole wheat—for the community and retreatants. Years ago, the monks sold their fresh bread to neighbors; the day-old leftovers from the bread route were reserved for the monks to eat.

Once the cakes are baked, they are set to cool overnight in a special compartment of the kitchen. Ultimately, they are infused with bourbon, wrapped in plastic, tinned, boxed, and stored. During the Christmas sales season, boxed cakes are everywhere, stacked and waiting to have shipping labels slapped on them.

"It's a competitive business," says Brother Raphael. Nevertheless, in a 1998 taste test, the *Wall Street Journal* ranked Gethsemani's fruitcake the "best overall" in terms of quality and value. That weekend, the abbey received 280 additional orders, some for multiple items. On top of the sixteen hundred orders they had filled in the previous three weeks, it was just too much to handle. The monks unplugged their fax machines and stopped accepting online orders. They were back up and running after the holiday.

The Miracle of Cheese

The cheese-making department of Gethsemani Farms was run for many years by the late Brother Victor Richert, an ex-Marine who entered the abbey in 1949, the year that *The Seven Storey Mountain* hit the best-seller list. He died in 1995.

In the early days of cheese making at Gethsemani, the monks used milk from their own dairy cows, supplemented by milk they purchased from nearby farmers. Now, however, with their cow herds just a memory, they make their cheese strictly with purchased milk. The trucks haul it to the rear entrance of the monastery. I still laugh at what Brother Christian LeBlanc said to me when I asked if he missed the cows. "Funny thing about dairy cows," he smiled. "Right when you're supposed to be in church, you're also supposed to be milking them."

As Brother Victor told me one morning, timing is everything with cheese making. He looked like the archetypal mess sergeant. He wore a white jumpsuit with a Trappist belt around his waist, anchored just below a slightly bulging belly. And he liked to talk. He told me about his background, as he worked, dropping details like the fact that his father ran a nightclub in Michigan. On the wall behind him, in the chilly, damp room, hung a painting of Jesus.

This particular day, the local dairy truck was so late that no cheese could be made. He took the bad news in stride. A demolitions expert in World War II, he had seen worse.

"After the war, I was going to be a CPA, but I couldn't get this place out of my mind," he told me. He stood with his hands on his hips, arms akimbo, grinning, almost laughing. The floor of the room was wet, and the strong smell of strong cheese was everywhere. A small statue of St. Joseph—"the patron saint of cheese," according to Brother Victor— looked out over the room.

"The best story is this," he said with a chuckle. "I always hated cheese!" He laughed harder, lifting his face toward the ceiling. "Me and Rafe," he said, referring to Brother Raphael, "we were in World War II, and we had what we called K-rations. It was always cheese!"

When he entered Gethsemani to become a monk and was told his job was to work all day with what he had learned to loathe, he did what he was told. He learned the process from the monk who was in charge. Gradually the work won him over.

"You get into the romance of grass," he said. He had been at the job thirty-five years on the day the milk truck was late. And yet when he talked about the step-by-step process—from the grass eaten by cows that produces the carotene in milk that creates the color of the creamy Port du Salut–style cheese that is shipped out from Gethsemani by the fork-liftload—he spoke with the enthusiasm and eloquence of a Walt Whitman. He couldn't say enough about the wonders of washing, salting, and aging cheese.

Listening to him, I remembered an observation I had read on the vow of obedience: "Often when we do something we don't like, we get the grace to eventually like it."

A Monk making cheese. Monasteries traditionally supported themselves by farming, but now more commonly do so through small industry. Gethsemani supports itself by the sales of its Trappist cheese, fruitcake, and Kentucky bourbon fudge. The monks make their Port du Salut–style cheese with purchased milk, now that they no longer have their own dairy herd.

On my tour with Brother Victor I had made some observations of my own. Cheese making is messy. Cheese must have time to sit, to rest, to incubate, to gel, to age, to grow in color. It needs washing, draining, smoothing, shaping, aging, cutting, shrink-wrapping. It's labor-intensive work. It's smelly work.

But to Brother Victor, the truest disciple of the Trappist belief in work as prayer I've ever met, cheese making is a true labor of love. "This is a miracle," he told me, holding up a wedge of pale yellow cheese. "Nobody, *nobody*, knows how it happens."

The Changing Role of Work

Fudge is Gethsemani's newest and fastest-growing product line. Inspired by a recipe donated to the abbey by a dentist in nearby Bardstown, it comes in two varieties: bourbon chocolate and butter walnut.

The fudge is packaged in boxes of various sizes, and the fruitcakes come in tins. But some of Gethsemani's cheese is packed in handcrafted, smooth-as-silk, round yellow poplar gift boxes, designed and created by Brother Julian Wallace. For more than thirty years he has worked six days a week, making these unique containers. With the help of an aide, the seventy-eight-year-old monk turns out more than five thousand gift boxes a year.

Brother Julian likes his job. He calls it meditative work, a quiet kind of handiwork well suited for a life of prayer and reflection.

But not all work at Gethsemani, or any monastery, is so obviously well suited to contemplative life. Work has changed in many ways, for monks and for the world at large. At Gethsemani, the labor tends to be less physical, more clerical. But perhaps more significantly, there's less of it. The workday is considerably shorter. Most monks, with a few dramatic exceptions, are expected to put in four to six hours of work a day.

That's not as it has always been. Brother Rene, one of the abbey's fudge makers, said that until about 1970, he and his brothers were expected to work mornings and afternoons. Today, work for most monks is limited to the time between Mass and sext, the noontime prayer service.

Of course, some jobs require much more time to perform. The work of a cellarer, for instance, is never really finished by the end of the day, as the work of a baker or fudge maker is. What's more, many monks pick up additional jobs that also take time to complete.

Brother Rene's interest in gardening led to his creation of a wildflower path through the woods to the Gethsemani garden statues, and to the planting and maintaining of young trees and shrubs along the way. The work often keeps him busy in the afternoons, after his fudge-making job is over. "In the afternoons, we are more or less free to do what we want," Brother Rene said. "The abbot asked me if I had time to make a path through the woods. I said, 'Sure.' And so I did. Most of it was an old logging trail. In the old days, we used to have horses and do a lot of work with them. So what I had to do was get the bush hog and drive down the old logging trail."

Father Matthew remembers the workdays as "limitless" when he first entered the community as a novice. There was so much to do, that it never got done. "We were into all kinds of businesses then," he said. "Well, it was more than we could handle. You know—the cows, the beef, the pigs, and the chickens."

He said that times have changed the abbey. "It's become very modern here, in a sense," Father Matthew said. "The advantage of capitalistic enterprise is that you can get a lot done in fewer hours. You don't need sixteen hours a day to do the job." He laughed. "When the corn was ripe in the old days, the whole monastery went out and cut corn for a month by hand. You know, one cob at a time, pulling off the husk and throwing it into the wagon."

Father Matthew is philosophical about the changes in work. You could say that he takes a Trappist point of view on the whole issue: a practical stance. "So now our business pays the bills," he said. "And we don't have to live off old ladies' gifts and old widows' remittances. And the interest from our bonds goes to the poor."

My experience, working on a history of Gethsemani in the 1990s, had put me in touch with Brother Joshua Brands, the abbey's archivist. Brother Josh's talents are many, and the monastery has used them wisely. He is an artist, whether weaving baskets of Georgia sweetgrass or designing an abbot's office. He is a thorough and careful archivist, whether preserving 150-year-old French legal documents or cataloging turn-of-the-century photographs of Gethsemani for the abbey's sesquicentennial celebration in 1998.

Once, watching his fingers move through the file drawers and cabinets of the monastic archives he has so meticulously cultivated over the past decade, I felt my mind shift to another time, another place, where another monk was going about the same business—saving the world as he knew it. That Irish monk, the monk whom Thomas Cahill memorialized in his popular book, would no doubt recognize a kinship with Brother Josh and his painstaking work in the Gethsemani archives. And with Brother Rene and his willingly bush-hogged trail through the woods. And with Brother Frederic and his annual financial reports. And with Brother Simeon and his fruitcakes fresh from the oven. And, of course, he would identify with Brother Victor, the romancer of milk, the monk who found miracles in the making of cheese.

5

A Gift of Simplicity: The Freedom to Be

I have perceived the excellence of God's glorious beauty.

—SONG OF SONGS

Slowing Down

At 12:15 each afternoon, Monday through Saturday, the monks of Geth-semani set aside their assigned work and follow the tolling bells to their choir stalls in church. Having left their computers and soup ladles and rider mowers behind, they gather for the ten-minute service known as sext, the Latin word for "sixth," a reference to the fact that it begins roughly at noon, or the "sixth hour" after dawn.

The trio of sext, terce, and none (a service that comes a little later in the afternoon) makes up the so-called Little Hours of monastic prayer. These three are shorter than the primary hours of vigils, lauds, vespers, and compline. Sext, in particular, is a brief interlude at the midpoint of the day, set aside for reflecting on what has passed so far and asking God for assistance to accept whatever the rest of the day holds. It is a time when monks pray for strength to resist being overcome by the demands and pressures of life. No doubt, most of us today can identify with that fear and that desire.

For me, a retreatant, the day still feels young when I stop to attend the noontime service of sext. Breakfast doesn't seem like ancient history. But for the monk, who has been awake and active since 3 AM, it's time for a serious break. He's ready for his big meal of the day, and perhaps afterwards a short siesta or a bicycle ride into the woods or a trip to the monastery's library to check out a book.

For some, the period after dinner is the ideal time for hobbies, such as gardening, or creative pursuits like taking photographs, weaving baskets, or throwing pots. Some may use this period to write poems, homilies, or musical compositions. Others will journal or sketch or paint.

Clearly, monasticism is fertile ground for artistic inspiration, and always has been. Benedictine composers took music to new levels of sophistication in the Middle Ages. Medieval monks also perfected the art of illumination, creating masterpieces of brilliant colors on the margins of delicate manuscripts. "That the abbeys have a number of monks with some artistic ability," Father Matthew said, "has always been more or less taken for granted."

Some monks so thrive on the monastic milieu that their artistry surfaces in more than one medium. Brother Paul, a published poet, occasionally gives readings at Louisville bookstores. The unofficial black-and-white photographer of postwar Gethsemani, he sells and exhibits his color art photography, which usually can be seen on the walls of the retreat-house dining room. He is also visible to visitors as the leader of the monastic choir, known as the *schola*.

At monasteries, inspiration for a monk's work comes from his life, and his work itself becomes a prayer, an offering of his gifts back to God through service to others. Brother Julian Wallace sculpts smooth, round boxes of wood that go out to Gethsemani Farms customers. Brother Simeon Malone is a potter whose clay cups and chalices are used at Mass. Father Chrysogonus Waddell composes liturgical music performed around the world. Brother Luke Armour plays piano and organ with grace and spirit. In addition to helping design brochures and catalogs for Gethsemani Farms food products, Brother Joshua Brands weaves elegant baskets of coastal sea grass and pine needles.

The work of these monks of Gethsemani reflects a larger pattern of creativity that weaves its way through most monastic houses. Surf the Internet for websites of Benedictine monasteries, and you will find that most communities have highlighted the work of at least one skilled artisan among them.

The Art of Prayer

Years ago, Gethsemani, like many monasteries, ran a gift shop in its gatehouse. I've visited abbeys, large and small, where you can pick up handmade rosaries or audio cassettes of celebrity monks giving homilies, or a volume of your favorite mystic's musings. Gethsemani eliminated its gift shop when the gatehouse was taken down and the entry to the church remodeled. In the future, a new one may take its place, but for now there is no retail store on the grounds selling cheese, fruitcake, or fudge, or for that matter, pottery or poems.

I like it that way. If you want to see evidence of the monks' inspiration for creating their food products by hand or their music, note by note, you can look to the sloping hills at dawn or to the mockingbirds at dusk or to the sun lighting up the church at noon during sext.

Or you can gaze at the giant banners that hang above the altar, or study the colors and shapes in the icons on the walls of the retreat house bedrooms. There you will find the work of one of Gethsemani's most prolific and talented artists, the late Brother Lavrans Nielsen. His story provides an example of an artist who was inspired by monastic life and gave back to his brothers and the world the fruits of his inventiveness— although his calling ultimately led back to the world.

Brother Lavrans was a monk of Gethsemani for some twenty years, from 1957 to 1976, when he left the monastery. He was by then an established artist. One of the first creative projects that the Brooklyn-born monk took on for the community was the redesign of the monks' robes and cowls. He then began designing and making vestments, the ceremonial cloaks and mantles worn by priests at Mass. Then he took up painting. He produced huge, light-filled abstract canvases in oil. He also worked in woodcuts and linoleum block prints, many of which were used for years as Christmas cards from the community to friends and family.

Self-taught, he was intrigued by Russian and Greek religious icons and developed his own modern style steeped in that tradition. He fashioned long banners of felt, depicting Christ and other holy figures, for hanging above the church altar during holiday seasons.

The monk in charge of Brother Lavrans's primary work assignment—the tedious chore of packaging cheese in plastic wrap—had noticed that it was hard on his spirit to be involved in such mechanical tasks. So Brother Lavrans was reassigned to the task of caring for the cow herd, a job he was not only good at, but that also freed up his afternoons for the pursuit of his art.

Eventually, he was given a hermitage to live in, with a studio attached and a quiet lake nearby. By 1970 he had exhibited at Louisville's J. B. Speed Art Museum and later had shows throughout the region. An art critic for the *Louisville Courier-Journal* called his abstract-expressionist paintings "extraordinary experiences."

He was forty years old when he left, no longer certain that the monastic life was right for him, and just fifty-four when he died. Father Matthew, in an introduction to a book of his work published posthumously, noted that Nielsen's art "continues to inspire" his brothers at the abbey as well as all who visit it. "May he live forever in God," said Father Matthew, "and not forget us who love him."

But the creative inspiration that issues from a life of quiet reflection and community support is not limited to the monks who live it. Visitors also can tap its source.

Inspiring the Artist on Retreat

At Gethsemani, it's not at all unusual to find artists of various stripes on retreat, either as individuals in pursuit of enlightenment and peace, or in groups gathered together for artists' retreats or workshops. Brother Paul has organized several working retreats for writers, for example, in an effort to link the act of meditation to the act of writing in a setting that is nurturing to both. Occasionally, artists whose work is tied to monastic themes come to Gethsemani to lead conferences or retreats on the grounds. Kathleen Norris, the best-selling author of *The Cloister Walk* and a Benedictine oblate, was the guest speaker at a retreat devoted to the link between poetry and contemplative life and attended by monks and lay retreatants.

Musicians, in particular, seem to find inspiration in monasteries. Cellist Michael Fitzpatrick of Louisville soloed several times at the monastery during the Dalai Lama's visit in 1996. Fitzpatrick was so motivated by what he experienced there that he went on to create a musical project called *Voices of Compassion* that has since been released on compact disc by his production company, Millennia Music.

For the recording, Fitzpatrick combined his own cello performances with the Gethsemani *schola* and the chant of the exiled Tibetan monks of Deprung Loseling, once the largest monastery in Tibet, numbering ten thousand monks. The music, a combination of Buddhist multiphonic chant and Christian plainchant, was recorded in the abbey church as well as at other sites around Kentucky, including in the Star Chamber of Mammoth Cave, a huge cavern about an hour's drive from the monastery, and at Furnace Mountain Zen Buddhist monastery in eastern Kentucky.

Fitzpatrick told me that his experience of playing cello within the monastery walls was, to him, like creating "miraculous music." The first time he heard the sound produced by his cello and the chanters inside the 150-year-old church, he knew he wanted to share the magic of it by recording it as part of an album. He said, "The more you play, the more your mind becomes drawn into the silence of the space, and the more your soul lets go of the pressures of the daily world. Even when the church is totally empty and silent, it seems alive with the prayers sung seven times a day. From this place true artistic creation is possible."

Extending a Hand to the Artist and Leader

More than thirty years ago Merton envisioned monasticism—and his monastery, in particular—as a vehicle for the coming together of artists and international leaders for the purpose of listening, meditating, seeking spiritual communion, and creating new perspectives on world problems. For monasteries to remain relevant, he believed, they had to open themselves to the world and its most pressing political predicaments.

In the spring of 2000 the Thomas Merton Center Foundation, an organization based in Louisville with close ties to the monastery, took the first step toward fulfilling that dream. An international retreat, devoted to the non–goal-oriented discussion process known as "contemplative dialogue," was held at Gethsemani for five days in late May and early June. The leaders who responded to the invitation were all advocates, in one way or the other, of nonviolence and social justice. The roster included thinkers and activists on the cutting edge of social change around the world, such as Adolfo Perez Esquivel, the Nobel Peace Prize laureate and activist from Argentina; Bongani Blessing Finca, a member of South Africa's Truth and Reconciliation Commission; U.S. senator Barbara Mikulski of Maryland; John Dear, director of the international Fellowship of Reconciliation; and Helen Prejean, the death-penalty activist whose memoir, *Dead Man Walking*, was made into a movie featuring Susan Sarandon and Sean Penn.

Gregory Acker, an ethnomusicologist, was also there as an artist–observer. Acker's artistic background is diverse, to say the least. He served a stint as a Peace Corps worker in Africa and as an artist-in-residence in Kentucky public schools. He is a musical-instrument builder, specializing in simple percussive and stringed instruments that he uses as a means of building a sense of community within small and large groups.

A newcomer to the abbey, Acker didn't know what to expect from Gethsemani, spiritually or creatively. He told me later that he came away from the five-day retreat with a renewed reverence for silence and a greater respect for the art of listening, both of which are essential elements in the making of music as well as in contemplative life.

Acker said the experience carried over to his relationships with other people, where he found that his growing desire to listen rather than speak was greeted at times with suspicion and resentment. He said he found himself growing less patient with the "tower of babble that passes for group process" in many collaborative work situations.

As artists, both Acker and Fitzpatrick seem to have been transformed, to some degree, as a result of experiences at the abbey.

And then there is Penny Sisto, an Indiana fiber artist who grew up in the Orkney Islands and is known for her haunting quilts, which have been shown widely, including at the Smithsonian in Washington, D.C. Her work often depicts the suffering of the poor and abused.

Sisto attended the international retreat, mostly listening during the conversations that grew up, spontaneously, among the leaders who gathered in a circle of chairs in the abbey chapel several times each day. One day, midway through the week, she explained she had to leave for the night but would be back the next day. She did return, but not alone. She brought with her a full-sized quilt brimming with unforgettable fabric images and faces embroidered to the cloth, all drawn from the conversations she had heard, all created through the course of a single night as she worked on them, piece by piece, at her home in Indiana.

Sisto is no newcomer to Gethsemani. She and her husband, jazz musician Richard Sisto, lived on a farm near the abbey decades ago when they first married. She has felt the influence of monastic life on her spirit and her art for many years. Still, for those who watched the process unfold, it was, as Fitzpatrick said of the music he heard in the abbey church, nothing short of miraculous.

Reading, Writing, and Reverence

But not all visitors are artists, nor are all monks. For some of Gethsemani's brothers, the time after sext may be spent with family or guests who come to visit. Some will catch up on correspondence, while others may have appointments in town with doctors or dentists. A few may need the afternoon to finish jobs they didn't have time to complete before sext. Others will meet with retreatants for counseling.

But first things first: dinner comes immediately after sext. This is the principal meal of the day, eaten in the refectory, or dining room, at long tables where the monks sit according to the date of their entry into the community. Food is simple but nourishing, and vegetarian for the most part. (Monks abstain from meat at their monastery meals but are free to have a hamburger or steak when eating out, especially if to refuse meat would inconvenience someone else.) The job of cook rotates through the house, like all jobs, and as one might expect, the style and quality of the cooking varies depending on who's in charge.

Prayer begins and concludes each of the monk's meals. At dinner they eat in silence, as one of their brothers reads a book aloud, a chapter or so each day until completed. This is a well-established tradition at many monasteries.

In the retreat house, dinner is served at the same hour, but there is

Blessing a meal. Father Damien Thompson, abbot of Gethsemani, offers a blessing before a community meal in the refectory. The monks follow a vegetarian diet.

no reading aloud. Rather, audiotapes of homilies or lectures are played at the noon and evening meals. Breakfast is usually accompanied by taped music. No prayers are ever said publicly. Individuals are free to pray silently at their places.

Some of the books read aloud at the monks' meals are straight off the best-seller lists. But the reading of secular literature was not always encouraged at abbeys like Gethsemani. Prior to the loosening of restrictions in the 1960s, the reading of novels, for example, was banned. As late as 1967, Dom James Fox discouraged his monks from reading fiction of any kind. "He would encourage people to read history, but the novels were kind of like underground," Brother Paul recalled. "When Pasternak's *Doctor Zhivago* came out, I remember having to go see the brother who was in charge of the eye clinic. I had to see him for glasses or something. He offered to pass along *Doctor Zhivago* to me, if I wanted to read it."

Eventually, a monk's preference in reading material became his own

Rear of the retreat house and meditation garden. Gethsemani's retreat house looks out to a meditation garden. The ground floor contains a dining room, kitchen, meeting rooms and lobby. The library, chaplain's office and screened porch are located on the first floor.

business. Today, the choices are wide open, and the official mealtime reading includes biographies and novels about lay people and secular issues as well as spiritual matters and religious leaders. For example, some recent books read aloud at dinner included *Into Thin Air: A Personal Account of the Mount Everest Disaster* by Jon Krakauer; *Wilderness at Dawn: The Settling of the North American Continent* by Ted Morgan; *The Color of Water: A Black Man's Tribute to His White Mother* by James McBride; and one by a fellow Cistercian, Michael Casey, called *Truthful Living*.

In 1990 I took my first tour of the monastery library, which boasts more than forty thousand volumes representing a wide variety of genres. I suppose I was expecting to see only religious titles and mostly old dusty leather bindings. I had to chuckle when I caught sight of a section housing musical recordings; among the composers I spotted were Vivaldi, the Ink Spots, and the Beatles.

Newspapers, on the other hand, are still subject to a certain degree of house censorship. Only news sections are put out for general consumption in the reading room, called the "scriptorium." There is, however, a not-so-underground sports section that has daily made the rounds as long as anybody can remember.

Today, several monks continue a literary tradition that began at Gethsemani with the success of Merton's and Father Raymond Flanagan's popular appeal as authors in the 1950s. At other monasteries, authors also thrive. Two of the best-known writers on contemplative prayer today—Father Basil Pennington and Father Thomas Keating—are Trappists associated with monasteries in Massachusetts and Colorado. Many Benedictine monks and nuns have also written scholarly and popular books on the subjects of monastic life, spiritual journaling, and prayer.

The Cistercians, like other Benedictines, publish several journals of their own, from the scholarly *Cistercian Studies* to a panoply of magazines and newsletters pertaining to specific interests, from liturgical music to the hermit life. Cistercian Publications publishes translations of twelfth-century monastic writers as part of its Cistercian Fathers Series, and a companion Cistercian Studies Series that includes both ancient and modern authors' works.

At Gethsemani, the torchbearer of Merton's literary legacy is Brother Patrick Hart, the monk who was his secretary at the time of his death. Brother Patrick also served as secretary to Dom James Fox and to every Gethsemani abbot since. For more than thirty years he has been intimately involved in Merton's posthumous publications, particularly his journals, as a consultant and editor. Brother Patrick has published two of his own journals as well: one written during travels in Greece, the other while in Israel.

Father Matthew has five books to his credit, including *Flute Solo*, a spiritual memoir based on his experiences as a lone monk in a hermitage in Papua New Guinea. A dynamic and eccentric speaker, Father Matthew delivers his homilies as if he were an actor improvising lines. His stage presence is evident when delivering homilies from Gethsemani's pulpit in a deep voice that resounds through the church, but it's even more palpable when he "performs" his after-compline talks in the chapel adjacent to the church each weeknight. "I was no good in sports as a boy, but I could act. I was always in plays," Father Matthew said. "And I could write, and I could talk."

As chaplain, he gets ample opportunity to talk to retreatants who seek his counsel in the private office he keeps on the first floor of the retreat house. He can often be found there, deep in conversation with a visitor in need of his guidance, or with someone simply eager to meet the man behind the homilies. He is as approachable in person as his homilies are accessible on the page.

He is a master of opening lines, the kind you can't resist. Consider this one: "You look at Salvador Dali's splendid study of the Last Supper and you wonder why all their heads are down, all twelve of them." Or: "Almost anything can be a way to prayer. Like a motorcycle." He never reaches for the lofty line when an earthbound one will do. Consequently, his writing comes across as authentic, heartfelt, no-nonsense, serious communication, written by an Irish American blessed with a streak of mischief.

Father Matthew says he writes with Trappist simplicity and a trust in God to get it right for him. "I just write it as it comes. And if I go back over it and try to improve it, I only mess it up, so I leave it alone. Usually, it's the first draft and that's it."

A Delicate Balance

On Fridays, in particular, the monastery buzzes with activity that's often beyond the control of the monks. This is, after all, the day that the midweek retreatants check out and the weekenders arrive. Hired cleaning crews must get in and out quickly, and there are always problems to handle: a retreatant who missed his plane, another's flat tire, luggage to be hauled in from the parking lot, special needs to be met. Murphy's Law applies in monasteries just as surely as it does everywhere else.

So stragglers sometimes arrive late to sext, hustling in through various doorways of the church, dipping into the holy water fonts as they enter, crossing themselves as they hurry to their places beside their brothers in choir.

In the stricter, more austere days of monasticism such tardiness would have resulted in penalties meted out in meetings that Trappists called the "Chapter of Faults." At these routine sessions, which were conducted by most monastic orders until the 1960s, monks were expected to proclaim their own and each other's violations of the Rule.

At Trappist monasteries, where the practice was carried out in a more severe manner than elsewhere, the abbot might sentence the offending monk to lie prostrate by the door of the dining room, silently accepting the humiliation of having his brothers step over and around him to get to their meals. Or, he might order him to sit on a footstool rather than a chair as he ate his meal. Such public "penance"—a system of punishments as old as the Cistercian order itself—went out with Gregorian chant and self-flagellation in the 1960s. It is an element of the past that even the most diehard traditionalists harbor few regrets about abandoning.

Today, as I sit on my wooden bench in the rear of the abbey church, I see the monks who arrive late for sext as well-intentioned human beings, just like me, struggling to balance the demands of deadlines and duties with their higher calling to love and mindfulness.

I find solace in their unsuccessful efforts, even as I find inspiration and incentive in the collective voice of their prayers, with which they turn to God at this midpoint of the day.

6

Together in Solitude: The Experience of Community

There is a relative peace in the monastery. But there has to be a certain amount of dissatisfaction, for the peace we are looking for is not on earth.

—THOMAS MERTON, FROM A TALK TO NOVICES

Going It Alone

Sleeping in on a Saturday morning is a luxury even the worst workaholic indulges in occasionally—but not the monk. For him, Saturday is a workday like any other. The bells call him to vigils at the same wee, small hour, and his job runs on the usual schedule.

Yet, there is a charge in the abbey air on Saturdays, triggered in part by the enthusiasm of the flock of fresh weekend retreatants beginning their first full day at the monastery, and also by the fact that Sunday, the Sabbath, the day of rest, is but one night's sleep away.

On a sunny Saturday morning, if you are on retreat for just the weekend, it is tempting to spend your quiet time in nature. The stained-glass refuge of the church may beckon. The library may tease. Your guest room, with its simple desk and fetching view of the monastic garden, may bid you to read or write or pray there.

But the call of the countryside is what I am most likely to heed on a weekend when the weather cooperates. I tend to take to one of the paths across the highway known locally as Monks Road. Depending on how I feel, I might take a sheltered route, one of the footworn trails canopied by redbuds, sassafras, dogwoods, and sycamores, or opt for wide-open spaces and wander a gravel or dirt road leading past barns or lakes. Whatever path I choose is, I find, the right one: it takes me to the quiet, solitary place that a monastery is all about finding.

Often, it's while walking a meadow or sitting on a meditation chair left in some out-of-the-way thicket by a thoughtful monk that I have my most meaningful moments of reflection at Gethsemani.

It's true of monks as well: many of them seek solitude in nature. As odd as it might sound, Trappist monks spend most of their time with other people. They live in community with their brothers: praying with them, eating with them, confronting problems with them, making decisions with them, singing with them, working with them. It is one of the paradoxes of a monk's life that he often struggles to carve out a place and a time to seek God alone.

At Gethsemani, however, as at some other monasteries, monks can be highly creative about finding solitude for themselves. Many create daytime hermitages out of abandoned toolsheds, empty corners of old barns, or modest cabins built explicitly for that purpose. One monk was known to live as a hermit within his own room in the 1960s.

Brother Paul, the poet and photographer, has been sleeping outdoors under the stars, winter and summer, since June of 1994. He camps each night by an old woodshed, a short walk from the monastery. He has a sleeping bag that keeps him warm on chilly nights. He admits, however, that its downy warmth is sometimes not enough to get him through a bitter cold snap, and he retreats indoors for a night or two. "I just feel more real out there," he said, by way of explanation for his unusual nighttime habits. "It's beautiful to wake up and see the

moonlight and hear the whippoorwills and feel the dew. It's health-
ier too."

It's true that breathing fresh air is good for the body as well as the
soul, but there are also risks to sleeping outdoors. Brother Paul, like any
camper, has had his midnight brushes with creatures large and small.
"A donkey once woke me up. I thought it was a dog. Then I thought it
was a deer. Then I said, 'Oh it's a donkey.' There have been some bea-
gles out there, and every now and then a stray dog," he said.

A few times, he's awakened to see a stray sleeping about fifteen
feet away from him. "You know, they like sleeping with somebody
around. They just kind of curl up and sleep. And if you don't threaten
animals, they'll just go their own way, and mind their own business,"
he said. "I remember lying down in bed one night and—this was in the
summertime—feeling this plop! I looked up. There was a frog sitting
right on my sheet. That was great."

A Room of One's Own

There was a time when Trappist monks slept in open dormitories, with
each one assigned to a cubicle just large enough for his straw mattress
and a couple of hooks on which to hang his habit. A drawn curtain
offered the only privacy. "The only place to be quiet and alone before
we had private rooms was the scriptorium or library," Father Matthew
told me. The constant interaction with other people was grating on
the nerves, he said, and tough on relationships.

Brother Paul recalled the days when monks who snored were
assigned a separate place to sleep, apart from their brothers. Jack Ford,
the long-time student of life at Gethsemani, said that over the years he
heard lots of stories about those crowded dorms from the older monks.
"Imagine what it would be like in the summertime. I still hear about
the nights when one man would lift the window up and the other would

get up right after him and pull the window down. You can imagine how uncomfortable that would be," Ford said.

Today each monk has a room of his own, small but private. The rooms are not air-conditioned, and the Kentucky summers are just as uncomfortable as ever. Yet, figuratively speaking as well as literally, they never heat up the way the old dorms did. "Getting private rooms cooled down a lot of the tensions that arise when you have a hundred people living close together day and night," Father Matthew said. "You know, everybody needs a place of refuge."

But private havens were few in those days. There were, for example, rules against walking in the woods alone. If your work assignment called for you to cut timber or clear paths, then you were allowed to make your way through the trees—with your brothers, of course. Solitary strolls were confined to the cemetery or the yard. A novice had even more restrictions on his movement. "It was considered a major concession, just being able to go out back, to the orchard," Father Matthew said. "Only very slowly did they begin to allow it. Some of the monks even bragged about having never seen the woods!"

For Brother Paul, today's private rooms and blanket permission to walk the monastery's thousands of acres are still not enough to quench his thirst for solitude. And so he spends his nights outdoors by the woodshed. "For me, there's just something about being solitary," he said. "I love being alone."

Private spiritual retreats also help ease the pressures of community life. Once a year, Gethsemani closes down the guesthouse for a week and holds an on-site retreat for the community at large, usually led by someone from outside the monastery. The Cistercian constitution calls for at least six days of retreat per year for each community of nuns or monks.

In addition, at various times throughout the rest of the year, individuals can make week-long private retreats. Some head for other monasteries, but many prefer to spend them alone at the hermitage where Merton lived in the 1960s. The place is far enough away from the community buildings to feel remote, but has the benefit of running water, a small chapel, a desk, a fireplace, a shower, and a modest kitchen.

When the hermitage isn't available for a retreat, some monks improvise. Brother Paul, for example, tells the story of the time he planned to stay a week at Merton's hermitage, only to discover that the place was occupied when the time came to begin his retreat. Undaunted, he headed for a remote section of the woods where he camped, without a tent, by one of the monastery's many lakes. When it rained on his campsite one day, he simply moved into the lake to wait out the shower. He kept his clothes dry in a plastic bag.

Some monks, like Father Alan Gilmore, have come up with creative alternatives to a strictly communal life at Gethsemani. Father Alan is what you could call a "day hermit." During daylight hours he and others like him take their reading or work to cabins they set up for themselves at various locations on the monastic grounds. They still sleep in their rooms at night and in every other way maintain the rhythm of community life.

These hermitages vary in size and character. Most are wooden sheds with just enough room to sit with a book or a rosary. They are usually located in a shady, isolated spot off a dirt road or footpath.

Father Alan's hermitage is on the site of a former pigsty. He calls it St. Aidan's Anchorage, after an Irish monk and bishop of northern England. He has thought of it as an extension of the monastery, not anything separate from it, since he first began spending time there on Easter Monday, 1968. The abbot at the time, Father Flavian Burns, had been a hermit himself, prior to his election, and he was understanding of the desire for privacy in prayer. In fact, Father Flavian's tenure in office coincided with a renewed interest in hermit life both at Gethsemani and throughout the Cistercian and other Benedictine orders.

Father Alan, a lay brother at Gethsemani for years before being ordained a priest, has continued to work at jobs that benefit the community. He was cook for a while and served two stints as guestmaster.

But he believes he was meant to have St. Aidan's as his hermitage. Years ago, he had a premonition of the role it would play in his life, he said. He recalled that as a novice, he once mired a tractor in mud at the very spot where the hermitage now stands. He had to get help to be pulled out. The incident proved to be an apt metaphor for the process of becoming a monk, of surrendering one's autonomy and accepting one's dependence on God, of being bogged down and rescued.

Father Alan's hermitage measures roughly twelve by twenty feet, a small but solid structure that he has renovated and restored over time, replacing the roof, repairing the windows, insulating it against heat and cold. Although he's never spent a night in it nor even stayed there past dark (it has neither electricity nor running water), he reads and prays in it. Depending on the season, he sometimes has to walk through a cornfield to get to it.

Father Alan, at seventy, is one of those monks, like Brother Paul, who looks much younger than his true age. Like Brother Paul, he too wears a beard, and has a warm engaging smile. When I asked him why a monk would seek solitude in a hermitage, he laughed and repeated a joke he said used to make the rounds of the house.

It seems that in the 1960s, the late Pope John XXIII decided to give a papal commemorative candle to two monasteries in the U.S., presumably one that belonged to a contemplative order and one that was part of an active order. Gethsemani was one of the two houses so honored. The joke at the time, according to Father Alan, was that "Gethsemani got the one for the active house."

Gethsemani was indeed a busy, industrious place at that time, coming out of a period of growth for the mail-order food business as well as massive renovation projects and new construction. Father Alan said that for the monks of that era, life at Gethsemani was like "living in a beaten drum." No wonder there was an impulse among some of them to seek private space in hermitages.

Father Flavian, now the chaplain of a Cistercian convent near Crozet, Virginia, said he believes the instinct to become a hermit is thoroughly Cistercian. A careful reading of the history of the order suggests that there were many cycles of "returning to the primitive ideal" that nurtured hermit movements. None lasted. Rather, there has been a continual ebb and flow of interest in "the solitary hermit" path, he said.

At Gethsemani, monks as different as Father Matthew, the poet, and Brother Frederic, the businessman, dreamed of creating experimental monastic communities, both on the grounds of Gethsemani and in other, more exotic locations. The two monks investigated one such place, a hermit colony in a woodland area near Oxford, North Carolina. Brother Frederic didn't stay, but Father Matthew did. The life at Oxford was simple and frugal: no habits were worn, no music was allowed, and the monks supported themselves by weaving fabric. Father Matthew stayed three years, then headed to New Guinea for an even more isolated life as a hermit.

By 1976, seven Gethsemani monks were living some form of the hermit, or *eremitic*, life. Some lived in trailers in the nearby woods, while others took up temporary residence much further from home.

Experimenting with Tradition

This "neo-hermit" movement was not confined to Gethsemani by any stretch. Benedictines and Cistercians internationally were showing interest in studying and planning alternative communal lifestyles, based on the solid Christian tradition of the hermit monk. Father Flavian said that the favorite precedent cited by his Cistercian contemporaries was the monk Roger, who was allowed to live thirteen miles away from his monastery in twelfth-century Europe.

Dom Jacques Winandy, a Canadian Benedictine abbot and Scripture scholar, had published a *Manual for Hermits*, which roughly outlined the lifestyle and rules that he and his Hermits of St. John the Baptist followed. Benedictine writers like Dom Jean Leclercq and Father Peter Minard also supported the movement, as did the Cistercian abbot Dom André Louf.

Merton, one of the spearheads of the movement, had agitated for a hermitage for years before finally getting approval from his reluctant abbot, Dom James Fox. In 1968, when Dom James retired, he surprised his monks by announcing that he himself would become a hermit, living in a custom-built cabin in a remote corner of the abbey estate. Sadly, the elderly ex-abbot was robbed, beaten, and left for dead while in his hermitage one night. He survived and his attackers were sent to prison, but the hermitage, empty from that time on, has fallen into disrepair, overgrown by a tangle of weeds.

Ultimately, the General Chapter, the chief legislative body of the monks and nuns of the Cistercian order, decided against formally defining and regulating the role of hermits. Instead, it was left to the discretion of each abbot or abbess to decide whether a monk or nun could become a solitary.

In most cases, hermits were assigned some community task to perform in their hermitages—"something to keep you sane," Father Flavian said. "When I went out, at first, I don't recall doing too much," he said. "Later I had part of a secretarial job, just a few hours a day. Other times, I sorted walnuts and that kind of thing. And I was available for members of the community for counseling."

Gradually, as times changed inside and outside monastic walls, the movement lost its steam. Father Timothy Kelly, the successor to Dom James, cooled toward the idea of permitting monks to live as hermits, citing his belief that the solitary lifestyle posed a danger to a Cistercian monk's calling and to the overall health of the community.

Although the experiments continued, today's scattering of full-time and daytime hermitages at Gethsemani are evidence that not many are called to the hermit life and even fewer chosen.

A Life on the Margins

Father Roman Ginn, like most monks at most monasteries, defies all stereotyping. He is not the typical priest, not the typical Trappist, not the typical hermit. He is, and by all accounts has been most of his life, a uniquely creative fellow with a profoundly spiritual calling to live apart, unseen, removed from the daily life of his brothers.

And yet he is as integral to the community at Gethsemani as the most visible of its monks. Father Matthew told me that Father Roman stands out as "an example of the success of the hermit life around here." He added, "Everybody kind of feels that he is testimony to the authenticity of the calling."

Father Roman, at seventy-five, sports a long, straggly white beard and a haircut that would look right at home on the cover of a 1960s rock music album. With his two donkeys, Hosanna and Hallelujah, he lives on a scruffy patch of land in a primitive, one-room, woodframe cabin painted "Fighting Irish" green. This hermitage of his sits a few miles out from the abbey, a five-minute drive in a pickup truck, at the end of a dirt road.

Once a week, on Sunday, Father Roman makes his way to the abbey to celebrate Mass with the other priests of the community and to pick up provisions for the following week. Usually he walks, sometimes with his donkeys, and other times he gets a ride from one of his brothers who drives to get him. When he makes the trip on foot, he takes along his red Radio Flyer wagon for hauling back his supplies.

The day I visited Father Roman, it was early spring and his donkeys were feeling rambunctious. They resisted being harnessed, shrugging and bolting at Father Roman's efforts to slip them inside the tangle of belts and buckles. He was patient and never stopped smiling as he waited for them to give in and comply.

He was wearing a Notre Dame University sweatshirt and brown trousers, held up high at the waist with a leather belt. A baseball cap was pulled down low on his forehead. Unlaced waterproof boots covered his feet.

He had not expected my visit when I arrived with another monk and some friends. He was reading when we pulled up in the truck, but he came out at once to greet us. When I walked inside his hut to get a glimpse of the place, I noticed a book lying open, apparently the one he had been reading when we arrived. It was an old, dusty book. I've forgotten the title, but I remember that it was written entirely in French.

Father Roman answered all my questions about his daily regimen and the physical rigors of the hermit life, but I could see in his eyes a twinkle of repressed mischief as he explained it to me. He knew, as I knew, that the spiritual rigors of living alone are far greater and harder to express.

He told me that he cooks outdoors over a fire and keeps his perishable food items buried in a root cellar outside the door of his cabin. He eats from his garden, which he plants with kale, turnips, beans, squash, and the like. He harvests his crops himself. The staples he brings home each week from the monastery include coffee, rice, peanut butter, and his favorite beverage, Crystal Light.

There is nothing romantic or idyllic about the setting of Father Roman's hermitage. The land nearby is best described as marginal: tangled woods, rough terrain. The cabin itself is as basic as basic gets. There's a mattress to sleep on, a travel alarm clock, a variety of candles and crucifixes, and a stack of shelves crammed with books of all descriptions, ranging from manuals on the care of donkeys to a Catholic catechism in Spanish. Attached to the room is a covered porch where Father Roman cleans his vegetables and prepares them for cooking or storing in the root cellar.

He has lived in this hut since 1990, but it is not his first stint as a hermit. For most of his fifty-four years as a monk of Gethsemani, Father Roman has lived apart from his brothers. It's his calling, and he has never had any doubts about that. Though he was twenty-one when he entered Gethsemani, he had already lived a full life, rich in friendship, travel, and satisfying work. He knew what he was giving up, and he sensed what he was gaining.

Raised in Denver, Colorado, he spent World War II playing trumpet in a military band. He shared a stage with some of the celebrity musicians of the Swing Era and was stationed in Rio de Janeiro at the time of the bombing of Hiroshima. He stuck around after his discharge, playing trumpet throughout Brazil, but ultimately decided that the musician's life was not what he wanted. He wanted to be a monk.

So he sold his trumpet to the best player he knew in Rio at the time and headed for Gethsemani. It was 1946. The noisy expansion of the postwar years had not yet arrived. Father Roman settled into community life.

In 1966 he was sent to the monastery at Miraflores, Chile, a community that Gethsemani had taken over. He spent three years living with the monks there, and another three years alone in the foothills of the Andes living as a hermit. He shared his niche in the mountains with a twenty-year-old mule.

When he returned to Gethsemani in 1972, it was not for long. Soon he was again living as a hermit, this time in the mountains of Mexico. His hermitage sat so high above the valley below that he could see rain coming thirty miles away.

Father Roman was a hermit in Mexico for eighteen years. When he returned to Gethsemani in 1990, he asked for the hermitage he lives in now. Despite Father Timothy's misgivings about hermits in general, he gave his blessing to Father Roman. And he did not assign him any community work. "I'm not here to produce," Father Roman told me when I visited him that spring day. "I'm here to be."

Father Matthew, who has lived as a hermit and knows the psychological pitfalls involved, said that Father Roman's life as a solitary has been successful because he has not looked at himself as holier or more spiritually evolved than his brothers—only different. "There were too many people in the past who kind of made that move to the solitary life, disdaining the community. You know, it wasn't good enough for them. It was something they thought they had to move beyond," Father Matthew said.

For Father Roman, the choice was not a comment on his brothers, but a matter of heeding a spiritual summons, responding to an invitation to walk the less-traveled path.

The Paradox of Diversity

In the 1960s Father Flavian told his monks that if each one of them followed his own unique personal call from God, regardless of how it distinguished him from his brothers, he would be doing as much to support the community as the monk who was performing a job essential to the abbey's survival, like that of cook or cellarer or novice master. "People took this as a liberation," Brother Paul recalled. "You know, you began feeling free to do things that might be different from your brother's way but was what you were called to do."

Though Father Flavian affirmed it in the 1960s, Cistercian life has been moving toward greater recognition of individual differences among monks since its beginnings in 1098, Brother Paul said. "This idea of pluralism in our community—it always existed to some extent. But after Father Flavian's statement, we felt supported in being different and developing our own spirituality."

The notion of pluralism—the acceptance of diversity and individual differences—exists in tension with the ideal of unity and uniformity within the Cistercian order. Sometimes the byproducts of that tension are painful. If you spend any time at all at a Trappist monastery, for example, someone will bring up the issue of the "lay-brother question."

Until the mid-1960s, there had always been two routes of entry into a Cistercian monastery. You could enter with the intention of becoming a "choir monk," which meant you planned to become a priest and live a life weighted more heavily toward public prayer and spiritual studies. As the name implied, it also meant you spent a good deal of your day in church, singing the seven offices, and therefore you were less likely to take on jobs that required long hours of manual labor.

Those physically demanding jobs were left to the "lay brothers," or *conversi*, as they were known for centuries. This was the other route to becoming a Trappist. As a lay brother, you did not engage in public prayer in church. Rather, you said simple, traditional prayers privately with the other lay brothers, while the choir monks were in church. The lay brothers referred to this tradition as "saying their *Aves* and *Paters*," a reference to the Latin opening words of the "Hail Mary" and "Our Father" prayers, the staples of Catholic lay prayer life. The lay brother vocation became a tradition in many monastic orders.

At Gethsemani, the lay brothers performed long hours of hard work, farming or logging or building or cooking. The choir monks studied and wrote and preached. Each group developed its own traditions and customs, separate from the other. Even the clothes they wore were different.

"The brothers were in charge of the kitchens, the production of the cheese, the fruitcake," said Brother Raphael, who entered Gethsemani as a lay brother. "They were in charge of the farm, of the milking, the cattle, the marketing of our food products, the packaging and distribution of food products, and anything in the work and mundane affairs of the monastery. They were carpenters, electricians, the laundry men. They were all appointed to their jobs by the abbot. In a real sense, the lay brothers pretty much ran the affairs of the monastery under the direction of the abbot."

The choir monks sometimes helped out with these jobs, especially those still in the novitiate. But they had other work to keep them busy, Brother Raphael said. "They had their theology and philosophy studies, and they gave talks. The priests were busy in the retreat house, hearing the confessions of people, giving spiritual direction, and things like that."

In 1965, as the change from Latin to English liturgy was underway, these two distinct lifestyles were merged into one unified vocation. From that point on, all monks who entered Gethsemani (or any other Cistercian monastery) went through the same training and were expected to share in aspects of both callings, regardless of whether they intended to become priests. For example, all monks would pray publicly seven times a day in church, and there were no longer any distinctions between jobs assigned to priests and those assigned to non-priests. All monks wore the same habit.

Today, few vestiges remain of the old dual system, despite the fact that more than half the monks now living at Gethsemani entered under it and remember it well. The one element of the lay brotherhood that has persisted in some communities is the praying of *Aves* and *Paters*. Today, while their brothers are chanting the hours in church, several monks of Gethsemani who, like Brother Raphael, entered as lay brothers, gather to pray in this simple way in a separate room in the monastery.

Otherwise, the twenty-first-century Trappist monk has become an amalgam of the two long-separate callings. And to some former lay brothers, the order's decision to do away with their beloved and unique tradition still carries a sting.

Changing Roles for Women and Minorities

The Cistercians are organized along a *patrilineal* model—that is, one that traces its lineage from father to father. Despite the talk of mother houses and daughter houses, the men's monasteries in the order have always held precedence over the women's convents. For centuries, Trappist nuns, or Trappistines, as they are known, were not represented in the General Chapter and had no vote in the election of the abbot general, the order's ultimate administrative leader.

However, that too began to change in the 1960s. Cistercian monks and nuns are now considered a single order, collaborating on all matters with "due regard to their healthy differences and the complementarily of their gifts," as their constitution puts it.

It was not until 1990, however, that Trappist nuns voted, for the first time, in the election of an abbot general. That election was historic for another reason: for the first time ever, a non-European monk—Dom Bernardo Olivera of Argentina—was elected abbot general of the Cistercian order.

And yet, women have always been a part of the Christian monastic tradition. The first Cistercian convent, the Abbey of Tart, was established in 1125, less than thirty years after the founding of the order. The first Trappistine convent arrived in 1796, shortly after the Trappist reform began in earnest in France.

Just 150 years later, in 1949, the first Trappistine convent in the United States—Mount St. Mary's Abbey—was formed near Wrentham, Massachusetts, by a group of nuns and novices from Glencairn, Ireland. Mount St. Mary's, in turn, founded three of its own American daughter houses.

Although each Trappist community of women has its own abbess, elected the same way abbots are elected, the convents also are assigned a "father immediate." This is an abbot from a Trappist monastery who visits the convent at least once every two years.

The only American Trappistine convent that is not a daughter house of Mount St. Mary's in Massachusetts is Our Lady of Redwoods in California, which was founded by a group of Belgian nuns.

Redwoods, which took its name from the forests that surround it, is the home convent of Sister Maricela Garcia, the Mexican nun who lived at Gethsemani for several years in the 1990s. "At Redwoods, our whole approach to monastic life is very different from that at Gethsemani," Sister Maricela told me during a long conversation we had one day while she was still living among the Kentucky monks. "We don't wear habits in the first place—nothing except the white cowl."

The nuns of Redwood are also more modern and progressive in some of their rituals and customs than other Trappist communities, Sister Maricela said. They make an effort to use inclusive and gender-free language, for example, in their prayers. "We change the psalms into our own prayer, not just say them the way they are. Our Eucharist is very much oriented toward what is meaningful for us, not just following a format. And we use sources of all kinds—Hebrew, Buddhist, Islamic, Native American, whatever—at our Eucharist. We use contemporary writings that speak to the theme of the Gospel. So our liturgy is very, very meaningful, I have to say."

Proving that diversity is indeed a Cistercian trait, the nuns at Redwood also stand out for being more politically involved than most contemplatives. Some of the sisters have taken part in protests with members of environmental groups, Sister Maricela said. They tend to draw a diverse group of worshipers to their Sunday services, including many non-Christians from the nearby San Francisco Bay area.

Coming from such an unorthodox monastic background at Redwoods, Sister Maricela wondered how she would adapt to Gethsemani and to living in a more traditional community of men when she moved into their monastery for an extended leave from her convent. As it turned out, the adjustment was far easier than either she or the monks expected. "For me, it has been possible to be here in a community of men because of the confirmation I received from them. That helped me see beyond the differences," Sister Maricela said.

Bonded by Love

From the start, Cistercians developed an organizational model and a governing style substantially different from that of other orders that follow the Rule of St. Benedict. Cistercian monasteries are founded on the principle of self-rule. Each monastery has a great deal of autonomy. The central authority of the order is the General Chapter, the legislative assembly of abbots that convenes every few years. The decisions made by the abbots are then carried out by the abbot general, the elected chief executive, and his council in Rome. He is accountable to the abbots for the decisions he makes between General Chapters.

But the abbot general has no real authority to impose his will on individual monasteries or convents. He can make a request of a community at, say, Gethsemani or Redwoods, but he cannot force compliance.

Cistercians also invented a unique "filiation" system that bonds mother houses to daughter houses and allows for orderly expansion. By requiring annual visits to each offshoot community by the abbot of the founding monastery (the father immediate), Cistercians maintained uniformity throughout the order—from styles of architecture and music to interpretations of the Rule—and managed to keep daughter houses from straying too far from the central principles of Cistercian life. Having seen what happens when abbots gain too much control over their houses, the Cistercian constitution built in limits to an abbot's power.

For all its attention to the details of governance, however, the constitution resorts in the end to a poetic, almost mystical, definition of monastic life. The various convents and monasteries are held together, it says, by "a bond of charity." The monastic life is described as "ordinary, obscure, and laborious," but also as an enigma, a paradox, a puzzle, accessible only through God's grace. The monastery is an expression of the mystery of the Church," the constitution reads, "where nothing is preferred to the praise of the Father's glory."

A Multitude of Praise

By 2:15 in the afternoon on Saturday, the workday is done. Anticipation begins to build at Gethsemani; a palpable spiritual momentum rises toward the Sabbath. The last of the Little Hours, known as none, arrives, calling the monks to a brief interlude of prayer.

Some chant psalms from choir stalls. Others say their *Ave*s and *Pater*s in a private room. A few, like Father Roman, stop to pray in their hermitages.

All give praise to God.

7

Welcoming the Stranger: Social Life

Just as there is small point in a monk being a celibate unless he has a strong sense of the male's profound spiritual relationship to the feminine, so too there is not much use in becoming a monk without an experience of the strong bond every human has with every other human.

—FATHER MATTHEW KELTY

Finding God in Other People

Sunday mornings at Gethsemani arrive with a festive feeling, an air of joy and hospitality. On Sundays, Mass begins at 10:20 AM and usually draws a much larger crowd than the earlier weekday Masses. Neighbors from the nearby Kentucky towns of Bardstown, New Haven, Loretto, and Nazareth drive over to Gethsemani to worship at the abbey church, as do visitors from Louisville and Lexington, both about an hour's drive away. This is fairly typical of Trappist monasteries. They tend to be built within a short drive of small towns, where their Catholic neighbors think of the abbeys as their Sunday "second homes."

All of Gethsemani's priests come together to celebrate Sunday Mass—even Father Roman, who leaves his hermitage to take his place on the altar. The priests prepare for Mass in the sacristy, a large dressing room in the wings of the church where items used in the liturgy are washed and stored. The sacristy opens into the space nearest the altar, known as the sanctuary. At the start of Sunday Mass, the priests process into church with the abbot, who carries his crozier, the large staff with the crook at top that is a symbol of his office.

On the altar the priests form a semicircle, praying in unison with whoever happens to be presiding that day at the hour-long worship service. Visiting priests and priests making retreats may join them on the altar if they wish.

According to the Cistercian constitutions, Sunday is dedicated specifically to "the mystery of the Resurrection," and is a day exempt from all but the most essential, work-related duties. "It is a day of joy and freedom from work so that the brothers may come together to share the Eucharist more fully and intensely, and zealously apply themselves to *lectio divina* and prayer," the constitution decrees.

In addition to offering more time for prayer and contemplation, Sundays provide opportunities for monks to meet with friends and relatives who drop by to say hello on that day of relaxation and reflection. After Mass, customarily, visitors and monks mingle in the lobby of the retreat house, sitting on cushioned benches or leaning against walls, catching up with each other until the noon bells call them back to church for sext, and then to their main meal of the day.

At Gethsemani, there is a dining room off the corridor that runs between the small retreat house kitchen and the much larger monastery kitchen that is called "the speaking dining room." Here, monks and visitors can share a meal and conversation without disturbing anyone else's silence.

Children are particularly visible on Sundays, running through the parking lot or sitting quietly beside their parents in church or on a bench in the meditation garden. Some bring bikes or skates. In warm weather it's not uncommon on a Sunday to find a gathering of picnickers—one or two monks among them—sharing lunch in chairs or on blankets on the front lawn.

Many of Gethsemani's monks come from large families and they welcome visits from children. I once took my son, Josh, with me on a warm-weather visit when he was eight years old. At one point in the course of the day we encountered Brother Rene, who happened to be riding a John Deere scooter. He immediately invited my son to take a spin with him, and Josh accepted without hesitation. As I watched the two of them putter down the blacktop driveway, their shirttails flapping, I could not tell who was having more fun: my son or Brother Rene.

No question about it, the social life of a monastery in twenty-first-century America is a far cry from what it was for the silent European communities of St. Benedict's day. With increasing interaction between society and the monastery, friendships with "outsiders" are more likely to develop and flourish. Though the fruits of this trend are more obvious on Sundays than at other times, it has become an everyday reality. And it can be a mixed blessing.

Making Friendships

Like every human being, the monk struggles with relationships. Like the rest of us, he sometimes works through his people problems alone; at other times he seeks professional help.

For more than twenty-five years, Dr. J. David McNeely was the professional who provided that help at Gethsemani. A Louisville psychiatrist with expertise in family and group psychotherapy, McNeely served as Gethsemani's psychiatric consultant from 1974 until the spring of 2000. His tenure roughly coincided with that of Father Timothy's abbacy. In fact, it was Father Timothy who invited McNeely to take over the work of Father John Eudes Bamberger, the psychiatrist-monk who left

Gethsemani about that time to become abbot of a Trappist monastery in Genesee, New York.

McNeely was an odd choice in some ways and a natural fit in others. His experience working with group therapy and family dynamics was clearly a plus, equipping him with the right tools for dealing with issues of community life. On the other hand, his Southern Baptist family background had hardly prepared him for what he encountered almost immediately. "I found the men that I interviewed were unique, very bright, funny, and not at all like my preconceived notions of monks as being withdrawn, somber, obsessive neurotics suffering from severe religious scrupulosity," McNeely said.

His consulting job called for him to work with the community's vocations director, helping him evaluate the emotional stability of candidates interested in becoming monks of Gethsemani. He also was to provide inpatient and outpatient care should a monk need psychiatric help. As medical director of several psychiatric clinics and hospitals in Louisville in the course of his career, McNeely was in a good position to make sure any monk in need could get the best care possible. "I think they liked the idea that I was not a Catholic and could render objective professional opinions untainted by Catholic theological positions," he said.

He joked that he did have some misgivings when, a month after that first visit, a tornado ripped through Louisville, devastating the beautiful park across from his home and wreaking havoc on houses in his neighborhood. "My first thought was that this was iiipunishment from my Southern Baptist God for getting involved with 'those Catholics,'" he said, laughing. "Fortunately, I kept going out to the monastery and figured out that I probably needed to come up with a bigger idea of God."

McNeely, who goes by "Dave" among friends, quickly developed a strong connection to the monastery, despite his earlier misconceptions of the men who lived there. "I enjoyed being quiet," he recalled. "Even on the first visit, without looking for it, I sensed a spiritual force that was more than the collective esteem that religious and thinking people had for the Merton tradition there."

McNeely began his work with the monks at a time when they were just beginning to adjust to social pressures within the community that they had not been forced to address in earlier years. "The rule of silence had been relaxed some five years earlier," McNeely recalled. "The monks learned that their harmonious silence was disrupted by the sound of other's voices, other personalities."

Meanwhile, McNeely, too, changed gradually. As his religious beliefs evolved and broadened, he came to see that his bond to Gethsemani was a vital step along the path of his own spiritual journey. "Gethsemani is like the old Buddhist adage that says, 'When the student is ready, the teacher will come.'"

He found among the monks a respect for Eastern spirituality and an appreciation for nature, two of his own longstanding interests. McNeely, a musician, also came to treasure the instrumental music and the chant that plays a large role in monastic liturgies.

In time, McNeely's wife, Wanda, became a frequent visitor, too. When their fifteen-year-old daughter Amy died in a car accident in October of 1990, both Wanda and Dave McNeely found comfort and strength in the friendships they made at Gethsemani. Several monks, including Father Timothy, visited the couple at their home, and one of them, Father Felix, spoke at Amy's funeral. "For so many of us, the monastery has become an entry point for serious spiritual inquiry," McNeely said. "We return again and again, looking for, and often waiting expectantly for, something to come to us that will help us along the path."

Although McNeely has now given up his psychiatric consulting at Gethsemani, he continues to visit his friends there. "I have learned that

Gethsemani is much more than a place in central Kentucky," McNeely told me. "It is an inner attitude—a *Weltanshauung*—a way of looking at the world, if you will, that becomes part of the seeking person, wherever he goes after having been there."

Returning for More

In other words, the contemplative view of life has a way of getting under one's skin. Barbara Sullivan, a special-education teacher from a Chicago suburb, would certainly agree with that assessment. Nothing about the way she sees the world has remained quite the same, Sullivan told me, since her encounter with monastic life.

In May 2000, she and two female friends drove down to Gethsemani from LaGrange, Illinois, where Sullivan lives with her husband and nine-year-old daughter. Although all three women in the group are Catholic, it was their first monastic retreat. "One of us was turning fifty, and she had always said she wanted to go to the Abbey of Gethsemani," Sullivan explained. "So the other one called and booked a weekend."

Perhaps because they were requesting the weekend that included Derby Day, the celebrated horse race that is a can't-miss event in Kentucky, Sullivan's friends were able, at the last minute, to reserve two rooms for themselves. Sullivan wasn't as lucky. "I was put on the waiting list," she recalled. "I felt that if I got called that a room was available, then it was meant to be. If not, it wasn't."

Apparently it was. She soon received a call confirming a room, and the three friends made their plans. "We were nervous about going, and everyone teased us," she said. "Normal people go out to dinner when they want to celebrate turning fifty. We were going to a monastery."

Sullivan remembers pulling into the abbey parking lot after the long drive down from Chicago, and suddenly feeling terrified and uncertain. Just a few weeks earlier, on March 27, Sullivan had lost a dear friend to cancer. She was still grieving and not yet ready to grapple with all the spiritual issues the death stirred up in her when she arrived at the monastery. "I went with the idea of just slowing down and reading and seeing whatever came of that," Sullivan said.

The three women split up during the day, meeting only in church, at meals, and at the end of the day at a designated spot under the trees on the front lawn. There, they would compare notes and share their responses to the peace they were experiencing. "I walked a lot. I took advantage of that beautiful library. I walked out to the statues. I would go for a run and listen to tapes. I went to the prayer services," she said.

A self-described Type A personality, Sullivan said she was not at all sure, at her arrival, that she could "do nothing" for a weekend. Would she need stimulation? Would she handle the silence? Her worries, it turned out, were groundless. "I don't think I ever felt that calm before," she said. "I don't usually use these kinds of words, but I felt my soul had been looking for some kind of calmness, and I found it there."

What she had feared at her arrival in the parking lot, she later realized, was that she would want more of what she discovered there. And the fear was real. "I want to get back for a longer time to do some writing and some serious reflection," she told me a few months after her first visit. "While I was there, I signed up for another retreat—five days this time, on my own."

On her first visit, Sullivan read about monastic life as well as observed it. She listened to Father Matthew's after-compline talks and chatted briefly with Brother Raphael. But she intentionally did not seek out monks for private conversations or spiritual counseling. "I wasn't ready yet to talk about my friend who died," she said. "But I want to next time." Her voice trailed off, and a beat passed before she spoke again. "I wish I could take even one-hundredth of a percent of their philosophy home with me and live it. The way they accept what comes. Their whole philosophy and reaction to change," she said.

Sullivan said it's been difficult trying to explain to friends back home just what it was that made her experience at Gethsemani unique and unforgettable. "People who haven't been there have a hard time grasping how special it is," she said.

Bonding with Monks and Other Retreatants

Ruth Peyton of Charleston, West Virginia, was like Barbara Sullivan— uncertain and anxious—when she made her first trip to Gethsemani over a decade ago. Since that initial weekend retreat in 1989, Peyton has returned to Gethsemani twice a year, a week in June and a week in October.

During her first few visits, Peyton, a Catholic, was not sure how to act around the monks, she told me. "I used to put my head down when they passed, so not to disturb them. I wouldn't think of talking to them," she said.

Today, Peyton feels much freer to engage the monks in conversation, particularly the former retreat masters with whom she has forged friendships over the years. Each spring and fall, she talks with them about problems, discusses spiritual issues, and catches up with monastery news. Because she makes her reservations for the same two weeks each year, she also has come to know other retreatants who share her routine.

Mostly, however, she relishes the silence of Gethsemani, and the peacefulness. She said it creates a sense of prayerful intimacy with God that she can't find anywhere else. "It's so easy to become filled with awe at the trappings of the Trappists," she told me the first time I met her in the fall of 1990. "But you quickly learn you have to pull back and say to yourself, 'That's not why I came.' And that's when you see the beauty of it."

Peyton said she first heard of Gethsemani as a student in the 1940s and wanted to visit then, but she knew women were not allowed. Four decades later, when she learned that the ban on female retreatants had been lifted, Peyton wasted no time calling for a reservation. "Brother Luke was guestmaster at that time," Peyton recalled. "He said, 'You're in luck. There's a cancellation.' So I took it."

Like Sullivan, Peyton signed up for a second visit before the first one was over. She said she simply knew she had to return. And she did—twenty-four times over the past dozen years. "It's part of my life now," she said. And part of the lives of the monks she's befriended.

Family Visits: An Annual Reunion

Colleen Prendergast paid her first visit to the abbey on December 27, 1965. She was one-month married at the time. She made the trek from St. Louis (a nine- or ten-hour road trip in those preinterstate days) with her new husband—and thirty of his closest relatives.

That December marked her initiation into the annual Prendergast field trip to Gethsemani to visit her husband's uncle Paul, known at the abbey as Brother Raphael. Colleen, who is a grandmother herself now, has not missed an annual visit since marrying Brother Raphael's nephew thirty-five years ago. And the family, as a whole, has made the trek every one of the forty-plus years he's been a monk. For many years, they rented a Greyhound bus for the trip.

Relatives of monks stay in rooms in the Gethsemani family guesthouse and motel across the road from the monastery. Most Trappist houses have such accommodations, since it written in the order's constitution that family visits are allowed once a year.

"The first year I went was the first year the family guesthouse was completed," Colleen told me, "and only women and babies stayed there. All the men—even the teenagers and young boys—stayed in the old monastery where the new retreat house is now. We had to go down to the monastery to visit Paul. There was one little room, and we had to take a turn to visit with him. I'm sure those days were really good for him. His mom was still alive. He had been there only nine or ten years."

In the early 1970s the rules eased and monks were allowed to spend time with their families on the grounds of the family guesthouse rather than in visiting rooms in the monastery. It was less formal, more like visiting in a private home. "I remember we'd build a fire in the fireplace and talk in a big room in the guesthouse," Colleen said.

In 1984, after decades of snowy December treks, the Prendergasts switched their annual visit from winter to summer. It was an easier time to travel, particularly for older members of the family who had a harder time getting around in cold weather. "Summer made it more informal and easier," Colleen said. "By that summer we were starting a whole new generation of little children, and they could run in and out of doors. We didn't have to worry about mittens. I remember years when we had upwards of forty-five people making the family visit."

I've witnessed firsthand the Prendergast family's summer gatherings. One of those visits reminded me of a relaxed family reunion. In the evenings, after compline, with the summer sun still hanging above the horizon, members of the family, young and old, dragged lawn chairs to the parking lot of the family guesthouse and formed a circle for story-telling and, hours later, stargazing.

Laughing and talking, they sat in their ring of chairs until way past sundown. On bicycles, rollerblades, and skateboards the children blazed up and down the paved hillside driveway that leads to Monks Road. Some nights they roughhoused in the spray of a hose, cooling down after long days of playing hard in the hot sun, and hiking through clouds of grasshoppers and up dusty foot trails into the knobs. "It's a good time to be together, away from everything that's intrusive," Colleen said. "You can just sit and talk and visit."

For Brother Raphael, the youngest of twelve children, these summer reunions are anticipated with joy. In his early years at Gethsemani, in the 1950s, the rules about personal visits and correspondence were much stricter and more stringently enforced. Novices didn't see or receive mail from their families throughout their first year of training. The annual visit was just that: once a year, usually on a fixed date. If a monk's parents or siblings couldn't make it at that time, they had to wait until the next year to visit.

Today, there is more flexibility. Families are allowed to stay for three full days with one travel day attached to each end of the visit. The monk whose family is visiting is exempt from his work unless there is an emergency to attend.

The Cistercian Constitutions describe the annual family visit this way: "The relatives of the brothers are to be received with the utmost kindness in a way consonant with the monastic vocation."

A Sister's Story

At Gethsemani, there are many stories of kindness toward families, perhaps as many as there are monks there. One of them was told to me by Chris Brands Ferdinand, Brother Joshua's sister, who lives in New Jersey with her husband and three teenaged children.

Like Colleen Prendergast, Chris remembers her first visit to Gethsemani as clearly as if it happened yesterday, though it was actually twenty-one years ago. Brother Joshua, whose family nickname was Chip, had just graduated from nearby St. Mary's College, and he wanted them to see the legendary monastery at Gethsemani while they were in the neighborhood. "He announced while walking on the grounds, 'This is where I want to be.' My response was, 'Oh no!' My understanding of Gethsemani was that it was cloistered, and you dropped your loved one off at the gate and he could write one letter home a year, and that was to his mother," she said.

This concerned Chris, who was newly married but without children at that point and very close to her only sibling. "You see, when Chip said he wanted to be a priest way back when I was a little girl, I had a hard time with it. My reasons were all selfish on my end. I viewed the priesthood as taking my brother away from me. It was our mother who convinced me on my own terms that it would be fine. She told me I would see more of him as a priest than if he had a wife and family to tend to. So I was sold. But now, at Gethsemani, my response was, 'Man, it took me all those years to get used to you being a priest!'"

She wondered how the monastic life would affect their relationship. He had always been her beloved big brother and best friend. "I was used to speaking with him every day, and used to seeing him all the time and doing stuff together anytime we wanted. Our love for each other is so unconditional, we are like soul mates."

She and her family ultimately embraced Brother Joshua's vocation and the changes it brought when he entered Gethsemani some years later. But within one month of his becoming a novice, they received shattering news: Brother Josh's mother was diagnosed with ovarian cancer. "I was still reeling from listening to the doctor tell us when I phoned the monastery to tell Chip. They got him to the phone right away," Chris recalled.

Father Timothy, then abbot, gave Brother Joshua permission to keep a phone in his room so Chris could call when she needed to reach him quickly. "When it was close to the end, Father Timothy told Chip, 'Do whatever your sister says. If she says to come home, you go.' But Mom didn't want him to. She was so damned proud of him being there, and she wanted him to succeed and she prayed for him always, as the monastery did for her."

After her first round of chemotherapy, Brother Joshua's mother paid him a visit. She was treated royally by the other monks and "enjoyed that to the fullest," Chris recalls. When their mother died in 1991, both Chris and Brother Joshua were at her side.

"My primary reason for visiting now," Chris said, "is to soak up every minute I can with my brother. All of the rest that seems miraculously to happen to one while visiting Gethsemani is icing on the cake."

A Tradition of Hospitality

Deaths, reunions, vows, anniversaries—the stuff of family life is also the stuff of community life. At Gethsemani, there is a long, colorful tradition of elegant banquets and open-air galas put on for visiting dignitaries or to commemorate important dates and milestones in the lives of the brothers. The twenty-fifth anniversary of a monk's solemn vows, for example, or his ordination to the priesthood is a good enough reason to pitch a tent and throw a party for the community. Governors, religious leaders, benefactors—all have been treated to Trappist hospitality at Gethsemani over the years. It is true at other Benedictine houses as well; welcoming strangers is a part of the spirit of St. Benedict's Rule.

After my history of the monastery was published in 1998, I received many letters from around the country, written by former Kentuckians who remembered the festive events surrounding the one-hundredth anniversary of Gethsemani's founding. One reader recalled that, as a child, she heard Catholic luminaries deliver rousing addresses at the June, 1949, celebration on the abbey lawn. "I vividly recall many of the incidents, especially the one-hundredth Jubilee when Bishop [Fulton J.] Sheen eloquently gave his 'Thunder of Silence' talk, with Cardinal [Dennis] Dougherty [of Philadelphia] in his long ermine cope," Sister George Mary Hagan wrote. She grew up in New Haven, became an Ursuline nun, and is now director of religious education at the nearby Fort Knox army base. Just as she has never forgotten her excitement at spotting the abbey church when approaching the monastery as a child with her family, Sister George Mary has always cherished the pageantry of that auspicious summer day.

In 1999, in honor of Gethsemani's sesquicentennial anniversary and, coincidentally, the nine-hundredth anniversary of the founding of the Cistercian order, a series of festive picnics and sit-down dinners for hundreds were held to honor and thank those who have supported the monastery's work over the years. The chapter room, refectory, and even the cloister walks were transformed into banquet halls for catered meals at tables bedecked with cut flowers and candles. Friends of the abbey from across the United States and around the world flew in for the festivities. Cars filled the front lawn and spilled across the driveway into a field.

An Extended Family of Friends

A monastery, like a family, lives on in the memories of those who have shared its stories and its friendship. Chris Ferdinand knows the tender side of Gethsemani's monks. Colleen Prendergast knows their generosity and their welcoming heart. Dave McNeely knows their surprises, perhaps their secrets.

Jane Thibault knows yet another side. Thibault is a clinical gerontologist on the faculty of the University of Louisville Health Sciences Center, where she is an associate professor of family and community medicine. She also happens to be a Catholic who, as a young woman, was seriously attracted to the Carmelite religious order and its tradition of strict silence and seclusion.

In the early 1990s Thibault spent three weeks at Gethsemani, conducting a series of chapter talks on aging. At the end of her talks the abbot invited her to return on a monthly basis to counsel any of the monks who might have questions or concerns about their own aging process. She accepted immediately and soon discovered that not only the older monks from the infirmary were seeking her help, but also many of the younger ones who wanted to know what to expect down the line as their parents aged.

For eight years she continued to provide this service, forming many close relationships among the monks. Although she has made a life's work of studying older people, her work with the monks of Gethsemani has thus far been purely therapeutic, and not research driven. It has been a gratifying experience personally as well as professionally. "I feel as though I have a bunch of brothers now," she said. "It really feels like family, or like very deep friendships. It's a gift."

Surrendering to Love

Hidden at the core of all these memories, these stories of bonds with family and friends, is a profound lesson in letting go. Letting go on the part of retreatants and families and friends, and also on the part of the contemplative who, by heeding God's call, is changing the world around him as well as within him.

On this last night of my retreat I am reminded that a monk's life, like all lives, is a litany of hellos and a refrain of goodbyes, a series of engagements and surrenders of one kind or another, borne in faith, hope, and the love of God.

8

Saying Goodbye: Fruits of the Experience

As the hand held before the eye hides the tallest mountain,
so this small earthly life hides from our gaze the vast radi-
ance and secrets of which the world is full, and whoever
can take life from before his eyes, as one takes away one's
hand, will see the great radiance within the world.

—MARTIN BUBER, *TEN RUNGS*

Clearing the Way

By breakfast time on Monday morning, my bags are packed. The sheets from my bed and my bathroom linens are piled in a neat, damp heap by the door of my room. That's the custom here.

The monks don't charge a set fee for retreat rooms; you are asked to pay what you can, keeping in mind that there is considerable cost to feeding three thousand guests a year and maintaining the retreat house and grounds.

But no one checks to see whether you've made your donation before leaving. The monastery asks only that you strip your bed and put out your towels for the laundry service to pick up. All rooms must be cleaned and tidied for the next batch of visitors, who arrive on the heels of those departing. Each retreat house has its own set of rules, but the "free will" offering is fairly typical, as is the expectation that guests will clean up after themselves.

I carry out this retreat-house ritual with a bittersweet doggedness, determined to be out of my room by the suggested departure time of 8 AM, with my bags ready and waiting for me to tuck them into the trunk of my minivan for the long haul home. I have put away my notebook, now full of titles of books to read when I get home and names and phone numbers of retreatants and monks with whom I wish to stay in touch.

I look around the room, taking in one last sweeping view. With my family, on vacations, we use this final glance about as a safeguard against forgetting a book that's fallen behind a desk or a shirt hidden in a dark corner of a closet. It is a hedge against having to turn around and scurry back for items remembered a half-hour after checkout.

Here, however, this final survey of the room where I've spent the last week on retreat serves more as a spiritual snapshot than as a safety precaution. I will take it with me as a visual souvenir, a reminder of how far I have traveled over the course of eight Gethsemani mornings.

A Life of Ritual

"Monastic life is an immersion in a sacred culture," Sister Donald Corcoran, a Benedictine nun, explained at the Gethsemani Encounter in July of 1996. I thought I knew what she meant then; I am sure I do now. "Benedictine life is a total experience of sacred places, symbols, and rituals that shape and nourish the contemplative disposition with tranquility," she said.

Sacred places that feed our spirits, symbols that nurture peace, rituals that sustain a contemplative attitude—in one week's time I've encountered all of these in one fashion or another. In my decade of

Cowls hanging on hooks. Cistercian cowls are received by monks at their solemn professions. The hooded white cloak, modeled on the work clothes of fifth-century laborers, creates a personal atmosphere of solitude for the monk who wears it.

getting to know monastic life as it's lived at Gethsemani, I've witnessed many more.

There are the monastic rites, for example, that celebrate each step of a monk's progress toward solemn vows. The first step is his acceptance into the community as a postulant, after six months of probationary residence. The Trappist ritual that commemorates this spiritual milestone takes place in church. The abbot places a white robe over the postulant's street clothes, signifying his new role as a novice within the community. He is given a religious name, signifying the new life he is assuming in Christ. It is a rite of initiation into the contemplative life.

Several years later, another ceremony will signify the monk's profession of temporary vows. At this point he accepts the black scapular and leather belt. When he ultimately takes his solemn vows, the monk lies prostrate before the community and his abbot in a joyous ceremony attended by friends and family as well. He receives the cowl, symbolizing his full participation in community life.

The Cistercian constitution spells out the official formula for profession:

> I promise my stability, my fidelity to the monastic way
> of life, and obedience until death in accordance with
> the Rule of Saint Benedict, Abbot. I do this before God
> and all his saints, in this monastery of the Cistercian
> Order of the Strict Observance, constructed in honor of
> the Blessed and ever Virgin Mary, Mother of God, and
> in the presence of the abbot of this monastery.

If you are lucky, you may be staying at the monastery some time when one of these rites of monastic passage takes place. If you are a regular at the retreat house, you could eventually witness all the important rituals and ceremonies—from one man's acceptance as a postulant to another's election and blessing as abbot to still another's burial among the small white crosses in the cemetery.

I recall, from my first visit to Gethsemani, watching a man enter the monastery for his first day as a postulant. A duffel bag slung over his shoulder, he walked unceremoniously through the gates below the etched stone that reads "God Alone." He was one of the four or five who end up entering Gethsemani each year out of the hundreds who inquire.

On several occasions my retreat has coincided with the death of a monk. Once I was there when the bells began tolling, calling the dying monk's brothers to his side to pray. That night I resisted sleep in order to slip into the dark, all-but-deserted church, where two monks were seated on either side of their dead brother, keeping vigil in the center aisle. Throughout the night shifts of monks would sit with him this way, reading alternating verses from the psalms. The dead monk lay on a simple bier in his Trappist garb, with his shoes on. It was a moving sight, one that not only affirmed the simplicity of monastic life and the intimacy of Trappist brotherhood but also stood in sharp contrast to the discomfort modern Western culture so often exhibits toward death and dying. The contrast to a funeral-home visitation, with its elaborate coffin, dressed-up corpse, and noisy background chatter, was vivid.

The funeral of a monk is a joyful event, capped off by a eulogy delivered by one of his brothers. As abbot, Father Timothy was known for his candid and touching homilies at community funerals. Without fanfare or exaggeration, he was able to capture the spirit and personality of an individual monk.

Father Matthew has also preached funeral homilies that stand out in the collective memory of the community. Some have been published, including a particularly touching evocation of a monk named Father Peter, a priest of the community who struggled with what Father Matthew called "the dark demons" of mental illness throughout his time at Gethsemani.

Trappist burials, which immediately follow the funeral Mass, are as simple as simple gets. There is no coffin, little embalming, and no

Monk mowing the grass in the monastic cemetery. Each monk's grave is marked with a simple metal cross painted white and engraved with the monk's religious name. Trappists are buried without coffins.

extended period of mourning leading up to it. In most cases the funeral is held within twenty-four hours of a monk's death. If the burial is delayed for family reasons or comes during a summer hot spell, light embalming may be necessary. One of the monks—the infirmarian at Gethsemani—climbs into the grave to receive his brother's body, which is lowered to the earth by his monastic pallbearers. The other members of the community gather at the spot to chant and pray.

A monk's funeral and burial are part of a continuum of life in a monastery, carried out for the most part by his brothers. This is hard for the rest of the world to imagine: The men who dig the graves and receive the bodies and tend to the sick and pray with the dying and sit with the dead are the same men who cook the meals and make the cheese and deliver the homilies and welcome guests. There are no outsiders called in to do the work that a family does for its own. These rituals reflect a deep spiritual kinship, but they also create social bonds and a sense of familial history.

The infirmary, a bright, airy addition to the monastery that looks out to an open, sloping meadow, has fourteen rooms for Gethsemani's elderly and infirm monks. This setup is intended to help them remain close to their brothers and maintain a role within the community. Some monks, of course, resist the move to the infirmary when it becomes necessary, while others avoid visiting it out of a fear of witnessing their own future. But the interaction between the healthy monk and the one in need of care can be a psychologically rewarding experience. "We see men grow old and die here," a young monk once told me. "And there's a sense of completion in that, which is very powerful."

He told me of his own experience tending to one of the oldest brothers, a man in his nineties with hair pure white and as fine as a baby's. The old monk was dying and had to be held up and fed by his brothers. "He was so grateful to us," the young monk told me. And I could see that he, the young monk, was grateful, too, for the privilege of caring tenderly for his elder brother in his final days.

Sharing in the Mystic Dance

Each spring, on the night before Easter, I drive to Gethsemani for the Paschal Vigil. It is an ancient ritual, played out in the dark of night on the eve of Easter Sunday. It begins with the Fire Rite on the lawn in front of the monastery and then moves into the church, where it climaxes with the Mass and Eucharist. It marks the culmination of Lent and, in fact, of the entire liturgical year for Catholics. St. Augustine called it the "mother of all vigils." At Gethsemani, it is a celebration that lasts for hours and draws hundreds of people from across the region each year.

Imagine it. Under the stars, surrounded by hills and woods and the sprawling monastery, men and women (and more children than you would expect at a service that lasts until the wee hours) gather around a bonfire.

The fire is built from cold flint and rock. In a deeply symbolic gesture, a monk strikes the two hard surfaces together until sparks ignite, then fans the glowing cinders into flame. Before the crowd's eyes a blazing bonfire erupts, shooting red-hot embers high into the night sky. Meanwhile, each of us in the crowd is given a white taper with a small paper circle at its base. All the while, a cantor sings verses of "The Song of the Rock and Fire," a haunting chant to which the crowd responds the refrain, "Forever faithful."

Once lit, the fire is blessed and then spread to each member of the gathering, from taper to taper, until the crowd itself becomes a ribbon of light. The paper circles catch the dripping candle wax and protect our hands as we move toward the church.

It is an austere ritual in some ways, but there is song and movement to it as well, and a powerful, almost tangible, pull from the woods and wildflowers surrounding the abbey. There is a third-century hymn that aptly describes this ritual as the first step in "the mystic dance through the year."

Once everyone's candle is lit, we proceed up the wide stairs leading to the porch in front of the church. Slowly we make our way inside, taking our places in the folding chairs and wooden pews. Hymns and litanies and other traditional prayers fill the next hour or so, leading into the Mass. What I learn each time I take part in this symbolic night of fire and song is how much deeper our connections to God and to other people grow when we share religious rituals.

"Send forth your Spirit, O Lord," chants the *schola* at one point in the service, "and renew the face of the earth."

The Paschal Vigil also marks the end of the Trappist Lenten fast. A central ritual of monastic life, fasting is integral to Cistercian spirituality and history. The relaxation of certain rules of fasting at eleventh-century Benedictine monasteries was one of the things that sparked the Cistercian reform of 1098, and later had a role in the seventeenth-century Trappist reform of the Cistercian order.

Today, the Constitutions of the order spell out the role of modern monastic fasting and its spiritual symbolism: "Monastic fasting expresses the humble condition of a creature before God. It arouses spiritual desire in the heart of a monk and lets him share in Christ's pity for the hungry."

Lent, the Christian period of fasting and spiritual concentration that leads up to Easter, begins on Ash Wednesday. Only one meal is allowed for Catholics on Ash Wednesday and Good Friday. Trappist monks are expected to follow an even stricter regimen on those days. The Constitutions state that monks "are to be content with bread and water or something similar."

Trappists abstain from meat throughout the year, and like all Catholics, they refrain from all food for one full hour before taking Communion at Mass. A monk must get his abbot's approval before attempting to fast any more strictly than that, as a safeguard for both his spiritual and physical health.

What Lies Ahead

Once my bags are packed away in the trunk of my minivan, I set out to enjoy the rest of my last day. Perhaps I will take a final walk in the woods or settle into a chair in the library and read. I will attend each of the services, ending the day with vespers. If possible, I will squeeze in a couple of conversations with monks who have time for a chat. Without a doubt, I will sit for a spell in the abbey church, alone in silence, emptying my heart and mind to God.

Leaving the abbey after a week immersed in its unique way of life, one cannot help but wonder what lies ahead for monasteries like Gethsemani. Once you have experienced the peace and the respite it offers, you begin to care about its future.

Truth be told, the outlook for monastic life in America is neither grim nor rosy. As Father Damien told me soon after he took office as abbot, Gethsemani is in good shape physically because of its healthy mail-order business, which is a solid source of financial support for the community, and spiritually because it is essentially "a house of peace" despite the diversity of its monks.

Yet, there is no getting around the fact that the numbers of monks at Gethsemani is shrinking and the average age rising. Around the world, this is true of monastic communities. Internationally, the number of Trappists decreased 10 percent during the 1990s, ending with a total of 2,512 monks in 1999, according to a report published by the order. Overall, the order has decreased by about 15 percent since 1940.

Most of that decline, however, has taken place in Western Europe and North America. Monasteries in Africa, Asia, and Latin America are actually growing. In 1940, for example, there was only one Trappist house in Africa and none in Latin America. Today there are seventeen in Africa and a dozen in Central and South America.

All told, there are now slightly more than 2,500 Trappist monks and 1,800 Trappistine nuns worldwide. The average size of a community has shrunk to twenty-five members, far smaller than in earlier years. But the Western pattern of declining vocations holds true for noncloistered Catholic communities, too. For example, the number of parish priests in religious orders declined from 22,207 to 15,829 between 1965 and 1999, according to the National Conference of Catholic Bishops. It is harder to generalize about the many other Catholic monastic communities; some are growing, some declining.

At Gethsemani, the "decline" is relative. Though there are far fewer monks in the house now than in the bustling 1950s, today's community of sixty-five men is roughly the same size as it was one hundred years ago.

Father Damien is sanguine about what some would call a "vocations crisis." He isn't sure how it will happen, but he believes that God will keep the Cistercian order alive and vibrant, and that Gethsemani, in particular, will thrive. In 1949 it was a sense of cultural malaise that prompted a worldwide surge of renewed interest in monasticism. Who knows, Father Damien asks, what will trigger the next revival?

Father Timothy, his predecessor, concurred with that assessment. Before he ended his tenure as abbot, he said there were other challenges as important to the community as increasing vocations, and one of them was the need to reach out to lay people. In particular, Father Timothy believed Gethsemani should share its prayer life with the outside world to a greater degree than it does now. "There are so many people looking for the same thing we are looking for," Father Timothy said, "and there are ways we can support one another, encourage one another."

And if, in fact, the developing nations are to be the site of monastic growth in the future, then perhaps the greatest challenge facing monasteries today is that of multiculturalism. Monasticism, once practiced essentially the same way in every house around the world, must learn to adjust to divergent social customs and cultural attitudes, Father Timothy said. In the past, when a community sent a group to another country to establish a daughter house, there were few concessions to such regional or cultural differences. "As Westerners we have such a temptation to think our way is best," he said.

Discovering the Sacred in the Mundane

As the day draws to a close, the retreat house lobby bustles with first-time retreatants who are full of questions for the monk on lobby duty.

When the bells ring for vespers, the evening service that begins at 5:30 PM, they bustle off to the church. I enter alone, knowing this is my last chance during my retreat to observe the monks and pray with them.

The word *vespers* comes from the Latin word for "evening star," and the service is celebrated, in winter, as daylight wanes. In summer, it comes as shadows begin to cover the earth and cool it. One of the two major liturgical hours of the day, it is a longer service than most, comprising a hymn, psalms, a New Testament canticle, a reading from Scripture, a litany of intercessory prayers, the Lord's Prayer, a blessing, and the Magnificat, a traditional hymn based on the Virgin Mary's prayer in the Gospel of Luke. Vespers is the hour devoted to thanksgiving, humility, and the silent recollection of the day's successes and failures.

After vespers, retreatants and monks disperse for their respective dining rooms. I walk to my car, thinking of what Barbara Sullivan said when I asked her about the lingering effects of a retreat at Gethsemani. Sullivan said she noticed herself being more "mindful" of her everyday actions and more attentive to the spiritual promptings that are easy to dismiss if you're caught up in the hectic pace of daily life. "Sometimes, something happens now and I think, 'Okay, God, I get it.' I feel like it's a slap upside the head." She laughed. "It's like God's saying, 'You are a slow learner, but I am not giving up on you yet.'"

Some retreatants return home to seek out centering-prayer groups. Some begin correspondences with monks. Some immerse themselves in spiritual reading. Some find themselves being more honest in their relationships with family and friends—even with God.

Others have told me stories of how a retreat among contemplatives enables them, once they're home again, to discover the sacred in the mundane. Visitors who leave Gethsemani after a week of participation in Trappist life most likely will come away with a greater appreciation for the symbols and rituals inherent in their own domestic and work life: the first sip of coffee in the morning at the kitchen window; the midday walk with a colleague; the peeling of potatoes for supper; the conversation around the table with family; the shower before bed in the evening. Done with mindfulness and love and faith in God, these are sacred ceremonies, too.

Making Our Way Home

That is the legacy of a week inside a monastery, a time spent in silence and solitude, observing a community of monks as each one goes about the business of making a heart for God. Arnold Stofile, a South African political activist who stayed a week at Gethsemani in the summer of 2000, said at the end of his visit that the monks taught him an invaluable lesson. He knew very little about monasticism when he arrived. As a Presbyterian, he had never spent time at a monastery. He was familiar only with the stereotypes of contemplative monks. The retreat opened his eyes to the heart of their lives, as well as to his own. "Their life is no different from any other walk of life. These monks have their business offices like we do," he said. "The only difference is that they take time out to sustain themselves in prayer throughout the day."

As I pull away from the parking lot and hit the highway for home, I keep track of the abbey steeple in my rearview mirror for as long as I can, until it fades, then disappears entirely.

In a world where fidelity and obedience are too easily mistaken for signs of submissiveness and passivity, where people move like the wind from place to place, where charity has come to mean not love but pennies tossed in a bucket at a busy street intersection, I find comfort in knowing that I will return to Gethsemani, and that the monks will be there to welcome me as a guest in their home.

A Monk's Day at a Glance

This is the daily schedule for the monks of Gethsemani. At other monasteries and convents times may vary. Vigils, for example, may begin earlier or later, and the times of the lesser hours are sometimes adjusted to allow for seasonal work needs.

3:15 AM   Vigils (45 minutes)
Reading, individual prayer
Breakfast

5:45 AM   Lauds (25 minutes) (Sundays, 6:45 AM)
Community Mass on weekdays
Thanksgiving prayers

7:30 AM   Terce (10 minutes) (Sundays, 10:20 AM)
Mass follows on Sundays
Work until noon

12:15 PM Sext (10 minutes)

12:30 PM Main meal
Reading and individual prayers
Optional siesta

2:15 PM None (10 minutes)
Chores, reading, individual prayer

5:30 PM Vespers (25 minutes)
Supper
Reading and individual prayer

7:30 PM Compline (15 minutes)
Retire at will

APPENDIX B

The Monastic Family Tree

- *Fourth Century*: Anthony of Egypt and other Christian hermits move to the desert to devote themselves to God in solitude, simplicity, and prayer.
- *Sixth Century*: Benedict of Nursia writes a rule for his monks, spawning a network of European Benedictine abbeys.
- *Eleventh Century*: Robert, abbot of Molesme, leaves his Benedictine house to establish a reform community at Citeaux, France. The Cistercian order is born. Within thirty years the Abbey of Tart, near Citeaux, becomes home to the first female Cistercians. The Carthusian and Camaldolese orders are also established around this time.
- *Seventeenth Century*: In 1623 a reform movement of the Cistercian order seeks a return to the strict observance of St. Benedict's Rule. Its monks and nuns become known as Trappists and Trappistines, after the austere reforms at the Abbey of La Trappe.
- *Nineteenth Century*: In 1848 French Trappists from the Abbey of Melleray found the Abbey of Gethsemani in Kentucky. In 1893 Pope Leo officially recognizes two distinct orders: Cistercians of the Strict Observance (Trappists) and Cistercians of the Common Observance.

Recommended Reading

The following is a sampling of books that cover the history, theology, and practices of Christian monastic life. They were written by modern and classical Benedictine and Cistercian authors, as well as by contemporary lay men and women.

Aelred of Rievaulx. *Mirror of Charity*. Cistercian Fathers Series 17. Kalamazoo, Mich.: Cistercian Publications, 1990. A classic work by a major early monastic writer.

Aprile, Dianne. *The Abbey of Gethsemani: Place of Peace and Paradox, 150 Years in the Life of America's Oldest Trappist Monastery.* Louisville: Trout Lily Press, 1998.

Bamberger, John Eudes. *The Abbey Psalter: The Book of Psalms Used by the Trappist Monks of Genesee Abbey.* Mahwah, N.J.: Paulist Press, 1981.

Cahill, Thomas. *How the Irish Saved Civilization: The Untold Story of Ireland's Heroic Role from the Fall of Rome to the Rise of Medieval Europe.* New York: Doubleday, 1995.

Chittister, Joan. *The Rule of St. Benedict.* New York: Crossroad Publishing, 1992. This is one of many commentaries that have been written on the Rule.

de Waal, Esther. *Living with Contradictions: Reflections on the Rule of St. Benedict.* New York: HarperCollins, 1989.

Flanagan, Raymond. *Burnt-Out Incense: The Saga of Citeaux, American Epoch.* New York: P. J. Kennedy & Sons, 1949. The story of the founding of Gethsemani, by one of its monks.

Fry, Timothy, ed. *The Rule of St. Benedict.* Collegeville, Minn.: Liturgical Press, 1981. A translation of the Rule.

Keating, Thomas. *Open Mind, Open Heart.* Rockport, Mass.: Element Publications, 1986. A manual for the practice of centering prayer.

Kelty, Matthew. *My Song Is of Mercy: Writings of Matthew Kelty, Monk of Gethsemani.* Ed. Michael Downey. Kansas City, Mo.: Sheed and Ward, 1994.

———. *Sermons in a Monastery: Chapter Talks by Matthew Kelty.* Ed. William O. Paulsell. Kalamazoo, Mich.: Cistercian Publications, 1983.

———. *The Call of Wild Geese: Monastic Homilies.* Ed. William O. Paulsell. Kalamazoo, Mich.: Cistercian Publications, 1996.

Kline, Francis. *Lovers of the Place: Monasticism Loose in the Church.* Kalamazoo, Mich.: Liturgical Press, 1997.

Merton, Thomas. *Contemplative Prayer.* New York: Doubleday, 1969.

———. *The Journals of Thomas Merton,* I-VII. Ed. Patrick Hart. New York: HarperSanFrancisco, 1996–1999.

———. *The Seven Storey Mountain.* New York: Harcourt Brace Jovanovich. 1948.

———. *The Sign of Jonas.* New York: Harcourt Brace Jovanovich, 1953.

———. *The Waters of Siloe.* New York: Harcourt, Brace and Company, 1949. A history of the Cisterican order.

———. *Thoughts in Solitude.* Boston: Random House, 1993.

———, trans. *The Wisdom of the Desert: Sayings from the Desert Fathers of the Fourth Century.* New York: New Directions, 1960.

Mitchell, Donald W., and James Wiseman, eds. *The Gethsemani Encounter: A Dialogue on the Spiritual Life by Buddhist and Christian Monastics.* New York: Continuum, 1997.

Mott, Michael. *The Seven Mountains of Thomas Merton.* Boston: Houghton Mifflin, 1984. A biography of Merton.

Nhat Hanh, Thich. *The Miracle of Mindfulness: A Manual on Meditation.* Trans. Mobi Ho. Boston: Beacon Press, 1975. A guide to eastern meditation practice, by the Vietnamese poet and Zen master, often consulted by Catholic monks today.

Pennington, Basil, ed. *The Cistercian Spirit: A Symposium.* Shannon: Irish University Press, 1970.

Taylor, Brian C. *Spirituality for Everyday Living: An Adaptation of the Rule of St. Benedict.* Collegeville, Minn.: Liturgical Press, 1989.

Ward, Benedicta, trans. *The Sayings of the Desert Fathers.* Kalamazoo, Mich.: Cistercian Publications, 1975.

Wilkes, Paul. *Beyond the Walls: Monastic Wisdom for Everyday Life.* New York: Doubleday, 1999.

Cistercian Studies Quarterly, an international review of the monastic and contemplative spiritual tradition, is another good source of information on monastic life. Subscriptions are $20 per year; the average issue is 144 pages. Contact the magazine by writing: Cistercian Studies Quarterly, c/o Our Lady of the Mississippi Abbey, 8400 Abbey Hill, Dubuque, IA 52003-9576.

Catholic Monasteries
That Receive Retreatants

The following list of monasteries and convents is accurate at the time of printing. However, be aware that e-mail and website addresses change frequently, as do phone numbers.

Most websites for individual monasteries provide information about availability of retreats. Retreat houses vary, but most offer both private and directed retreats year round, as guest rooms are available. On a directed retreat you will meet regularly with a spiritual director. Most retreat houses are open to men and women of all faiths and invite retreatants to join their communities for public monastic prayer and to attend the Eucharist daily.

A general Benedictine website with links to individual houses can be found at the following address: http://www.osb.org/retreats/index.html. A similar Cistercian website can be found at the following address: http://www.ocso.org.

Trappist Monasteries and Convents in the United States

(This listing gives a description of each abbey and its Trappist lineage.)

Santa Rita Abbey
HC 1, Box 929
Sonoita, AZ 85637-9705
(520) 455-5595
Fax: (520) 455-5770
Founded by the Wrentham nuns in 1972, this small monastery sits in the foothills of the Santa Rita Mountains, near the town of Sonoita, thirty-five miles southeast of Tucson.

New Clairvaux Abbey
P.O. Box 80
Vina, CA 96092-0080
(530) 839-2161
Fax: (916) 839-2332
trappist@maxinet.com
http://www.maxinet.com/trappist
In 1955 Gethsemani made its fifth foundation in the valley of the Sacramento River, one hundred miles north of Sacramento. New Clairvaux, in turn, has two daughter houses, Our Lady of Joy in Hong Kong, and Holy Mother of God in Taiwan.

Redwoods Monastery
18104 Briceland Thorn Rd.
Whitethorn, CA 95589
(707) 986-7419
Founded in 1962 by four Trappistine nuns from Belgium, this small community in the redwood forests is near the Pacific coast, one hundred miles south of Cape Mendocino.

St. Benedict's Abbey
1012 Monastery Rd.
Snowmass, CO 81654-9399
(970) 927-3311
Fax: (970) 927-3399

http://www.snowmass.org
In 1956 monks from St. Joseph's Abbey founded St. Benedict's at
Snowmass, in the Rocky Mountains near Aspen.

Monastery of the Holy Spirit
2625 Highway 212 SW
Conyers, GA 30094-4044
(770) 483-8705
Fax: (770) 760-0989
In 1944 monks from Gethsemani Abbey made this, their first foundation, on an old cotton plantation called Honey Creek, near Conyers,
forty miles from Atlanta.

Our Lady of the Mississippi Valley
8400 Abbey Hill
Dubuque, IA 52003-9501
(319) 582-2595
Fax: (319) 582-5511
http://www.osb.org/cist/olm
Founded in 1964 by the Wrentham community, the convent overlooks the Mississippi River, south of Dubuque. The community has
its own daughter house in Norway.

New Melleray Abbey
6500 Melleray Circle
Peosta, IA 52068
(319) 588-2319
Fax: (319) 588-4117
http://www.osb.org/cist/melleray
In 1849 Irish monks from Mount Melleray founded this monastery
in the rich farmland of Iowa, near Dubuque.

Abbey of Gethsemani
3642 Monks Rd.
Trappist, KY 40051-6152
(502) 549-3117
Fax: (502) 549-4124
www.monks.org
Founded in 1848 by monks from Melleray Abbey in France, the

monastery sits among the rolling hills of Kentucky, south of Louisville, near Bardstown.

St. Joseph's Abbey
167 N. Spencer Rd.
Spencer, MA 01562-1233
(508) 885-8700
Fax: (508) 885-8701
http://www.spencerabbey.org
In 1825 French monks from La Trappe founded Petit Clairvaux in Nova Scotia. After a devastating fire, the monks built Abbey of Our Lady of the Valley in Providence, Rhode Island. In 1950, after another fire, the monks moved to St. Joseph's Abbey in Massachusetts, ten miles from Worcester.

Mount St. Mary's Abbey
300 Arnold St.
Wrentham, MA 02093
(508) 528-1282
Fax: (508) 528-5360
hospitality@msmabbey.org
This is the oldest Trappistine convent in the United States, founded in 1949 by nuns from St. Mary's Abbey in Glencairn, Ireland. It is located near the three-hundred-year-old town of Wrentham, Massachusetts.

Assumption Abbey
RR 5, Box 1056
Ava, MO 65608-9142
(417) 683-5110
Fax: (417) 683-5658
assumptionabbey@usa.net
http://www.assumptionabbey.org
In 1950 monks from New Melleray made their first foundation in the Ozark Mountains in south-central Missouri, near Springfield.

Genesee Abbey
P.O. Box 900
Piffard, NY 14533-0900
(716) 243-0660

Fax: (716) 243-4816
abbeygen@frontiernet.net
www.rc.net/org/geneseeabbey
In 1951 Gethsemani formed its fourth foundation in the Genesee
River valley of New York State, thirty miles south of Rochester.

Guadalupe Abbey
Box 97
Lafayette, OR 97127
(503) 852-7174
Fax: (503) 852-7748
community@trappistabbey.org
www.trappistabbey.org
In 1948 Our Lady of the Valley made its first foundation at Pecos,
New Mexico. In 1955 the monks relocated to Lafayette, Oregon, and
named their new monastery Abbey of Our Lady of Guadalupe.

Mepkin Abbey
1098 Mepkin Abbey Rd.
Moncks Corner, SC 29461-4796
(843) 761-8509
Fax: (843) 761-6719
http://www.mepkinabbey.org
In 1949 Gethsemani founded this monastery on land donated by
Henry and Clare Boothe Luce. It overlooks the Cooper River, twenty
miles from Charleston.

Abbey of the Holy Trinity
1250 South 9500 East
Huntsville, UT 84317
(801) 745-3784
Fax: (801) 745-6430
In 1947 monks from Gethsemani established this monastery in a fer-
tile basin of the Wasatch range of the Rocky Mountains, near Salt
Lake City, Utah.

Holy Cross Abbey
901 Cool Spring Ln.
RR 2, Box 3870
Berryville, VA 22611-2700

(540) 955-1425
Fax: (540) 955-1356
http://www.holycrossabbeybrryvlle.org
In 1950, shortly before Our Lady of the Valley moved to St. Joseph's
Abbey, thirty monks traveled to the Blue Ridge Mountains of Virginia
to establish Holy Cross Abbey on the Shenandoah River, sixty miles
west of Washington, D.C.

Order of Saint Benedict
Association of Benedictine Retreat Centers

The following is a list of other Benedictine monasteries that receive
retreatants. Many have websites where more information about
accommodations, fees, and reservations is available.

Canada

British Columbia

Bethlehem Retreat Centre
2371 Arbot Rd.
Nanaimo, BC Canada V9R 6S9
(250) 754-3254
Fax: (250) 753-6742
www.osb.org/retreats/index.html
Bethret@islandnet.com

Manitoba

St. Benedict's Retreat and Conference Center
225 Masters Ave.
Winnipeg, MB Canada R4A 2A1
(204) 338-4601
Fax: (204) 339-8775
stbens@mb.sympatico.ca
www3.mb.sympatico.ca/~stbens

United States

Alabama

St. Bernard Abbey and Retreat Center
1600 St. Bernard Dr. SE
Cullman, AL 35055
(256) 734-3946
Fax: (256) 734-2925
Shmon@hiwaay.net

Arizona

Tolomei Retreat House
Holy Trinity Monastery
P.O. Box 298
St. David, AZ 85630-0298
(520) 720-4016 or 520-720-4642, ext.17
Fax: (520) 720-4202
trinitylib@theriver.com

Arkansas

St. Scholastica Center
P.O. Box 3489
Fort Smith, AR 72913
(501) 783-1135
scholast@ipa.net
www.catholic-church.org/scholastica/

Hesychia House of Prayer
204 St. Scholastica Rd.
New Blaine, AR 72851
(501) 938-7375
www.catholic-church.org/scholastica/heyschia.htm

Coury House
Subiaco Abbey
340 N. Subiaco Ave.
Subiaco, AR 72865
coury_hs@catholic.org
http://www.subi.org/couryhouse.htm

California

Prince of Peace Abbey
650 Benet Hill Rd.
Oceanside, CA 92054
(760) 430-1305

St. Andrew's Abbey
31001 N. Valyermo Rd.
P.O. Box 40
Valyermo, CA 93563
(661) 944-2178
Fax: (661) 944-1076
www.valyermo.com
moks@valyermo.com

Colorado

Holy Cross Abbey
2951 Highway 50
Canon City, CO 81212
(719) 275-8631
Fax: (719) 275-7125
abbot@holycrossabbey.org
www.holycrossabbey.org

Benet Pines Retreat Center
15780 Highway 83
Colorado Springs, CO 80921
(719) 495-2574
bpines@usa.net

Center at Benet Hill Monastery
2577 N. Chelton Rd.
Colorado Springs, CO 80909
(719) 473-6184

Abbey of St. Walburga
32109 North U.S. Highway 287
Virginia Dale, CO 80536-8942

(970) 472-0612
Fax: (970) 484-4342
retreats@walburga.org
www.walburga.org

Connecticut

The Hermitage of the Dayspring
9 Beardsley Rd.
Kent, CT 06757
(860) 354-8727
dayspringosb@snet.net

Florida

St. Leo Abbey Retreat Center
P.O. Box 2350
St. Leo, FL 33574
(352) 588-2009

Idaho

St. Gertrude's Retreat Center
Monastery of St. Gertrude
HC 3, Box 121
Cottonwood, ID 83522-9408
(208) 962-3224
Fax: (208) 962-7212
retreat@camasnet.com
www.rc.net/boise/st_gertrude/retreats.html

Illinois

Saint Benedict's Abbey
(Ecumenical)
7561 West Lancaster Rd.
Bartonville, IL 61607
(309) 633-0057
Fax: (309) 633-0058
sbabbey@ocslink.com
sbabbey.com

St. Joseph's Loft
Monastery of the Holy Cross
3111 S. Aberdeen St.
Chicago, IL 60608-6503
(773) 927-7424
Toll free: (888) 539-4261
Fax: (773) 927-5734
porter@chicagomonk.org
www.chicagomonk.org

Indiana

Benedict Inn Retreat & Conference Center
1402 Southern Ave.
Beech Grove, IN 46107
(317) 788-7581
Fax: (317) 782-3142
www.benedictinn.org

Kordes Enrichment Center
814 E. 14th St.
Ferdinand, IN 47532
(812) 367-2777 and (800) 880-2777
Fax: (812) 367-2313
kordes@thedome.org
www.thedome.org/kordes

The Guest House
Saint Meinrad Archabbey
St. Meinrad, IN 47577
(812) 357-6585
Toll free: (800) 581-6905
www.saintmeinrad.edu

Iowa

Covenant Monastery
1128 1100th St.
Harlan, IA 51537-4900
(712) 755-2004
lzahner@fmctc.com

Kansas

Benedictine Retreat Ministry
1020 North Second St.
Atchison, KS 66002
www.benedictine.edu/abbey

Sophia Center
Benedictine Sisters of Mount St. Scholastica
751 South Eighth St.
Atchison, KS 66002
jkputnam@juno.com
www.benedictine.edu/Sophia.html

Kentucky

Mt. Tabor Retreat Center
150 Mt. Tabor Rd.
Martin, KY 41649
(606) 886-9624
mtbenedictine@pcc-uky.campuscwix.net

Louisiana

Abbey Christian Life Center
St. Joseph Abbey
St. Benedict, LA 70457
(504) 892-3473
www.stjosephabbey.org

Massachusetts

Retreat Program
Glastonbury Abbey
16 Hull St.
Hingham, MA 02043
(781) 749-2155
Office@glastonburyabbey.org
www.glastonburyabbey.org

Minnesota

Spiritual Life Program
Saint John's Abbey
Collegeville, MN 56321-2015
(320) 363-3929
Fax (320) 363-2504
SpirLife@csbsju.edu
www.sja.osb.org/slp

Mount St. Benedict Center
620 Summit Ave.
Crookston, MN 56716
(218) 281-3441
Amgeray@msb.net

McCabe Renewal Center
2125 Abbotsford Ave.
Duluth, MN 55803
(218) 724-5266
Fax: (218) 724-7138
McCabeRenCtr@aol.com

Spirituality Center
Saint Benedict's Monastery
104 Chapel Ln.
St. Joseph, MN 56374-0220
(320) 363-7114
Fax: (320) 363-7173
www.sbm.osb.org/spiritc.html

Benedictine Center of St. Paul's Monastery
2675 E. Larpenteur Ave.
St. Paul, MN 55109
(651) 777-7251
Valcarcel@worldnet.att.net

Nebraska

St. Benedict Center
St. Benedict Rd.
P.O. Box 528
Schuyler, NE 68661-0528
(402) 352-8819
Fax: (402) 352-8884
Benedict.center@alltel.net
www.megavision.com/benedict

New Jersey

Benedictine Center for Spirituality
St. Walburga Monastery
851 North Broad St.
Elizabeth, NJ 07208
(908) 353-3028
MaritaOSB@aol.com
www.catholic-forum.com/bensisnj

St Mary's Abbey Retreat Center
230 Mendham Rd.
Morristown, NJ 07960
(973) 538-3231, ext. 2100
www.osbmonks.org

New Mexico

Pecos Benedictine Monastery
Monks of Our Lady of Guadalupe Abbey
Sisters of Mother of Mercy and Peace Monastery
P.O. Box 1080
Pecos, NM 87552-1080
(505) 757-6415
Guestmaster@pecos-nm.com
www.pecosabbey.org

New York

Mount Saviour Monastery
231 Monastery Rd.
Pine City, NY 14871-9787
(607) 734-1688
Fax: (607) 734-1689
MSaviour@juno.com
www.servtech.com/~msaviour

North Dakota

Benedictine Spirituality Center
Sacred Heart Monastery
8969 Highway 10
Box 364
Richardton, ND 58652
(701) 974-2121
Fax: (701) 974-2124
home@sacredheartmonastery.com
www.rc.net/bismarck/shm/spirituality.html

Oklahoma

Benedictine Spirituality Center
Red Plains Monastery
728 Richland Rd., SW
Piedmont, OK 73078-9324
(405) 373-4565
osbokc@ionet.net
www.geocities.com/Wellesley/6285

Oregon

Shalom Prayer Center
Queen of Angels Monastery
840 S. Main St.
Mt. Angel, OR 97362
(503) 845-6773
shalom@open.org
www.open.org/shalom

Mt. Angel Abbey Retreat
St. Benedict, OR 97373
(503) 845-3030
www.mtangel.edu

Pennsylvania

Glinodo Center
6270 E. Lake Rd.
Erie, PA 16511
(814) 899-4584
glinodo@glinodo.org
www.glinodo.org

South Dakota

Blue Cloud Abbey Retreat Center
P.O. Box 98
Marvin, SD 57251
(605) 398-9200
Fax: (605) 398-9201
Abbey@bluecloud.org
www.bluecloud.org

Benedictine Ministry Outreach
Saint Benedict's
415 South Crow St.
Pierre, SD 57501
(605) 224-0969
bennii@sd.cybernex.net

Mother of God Monastery
110 28th Ave. SE
Watertown, SD 57201
(605) 882-6631
Fax: (605) 882-6658
sisteremily@hotmail.com
www.dailypost.com/monastery

Spirituality Center
Sacred Heart Monastery
1008 West Eighth St.
Yankton, SD 57078
(605) 668-6000

Texas

Omega Center
216 W. Highland
Boerne, TX 78006
(830) 816-8471
omegactr@boernenet.com

Benedictine Retreat Center
Corpus Christi Abbey
HCR 2, Box 6300
Sandia, TX 78383
(361) 547-9797
CCAbbeyRetreats@yahoo.com
www.borg.com/~paperina

Utah

Our Lady of the Mountain Retreat House
1794 Lake St.
Ogden, UT 84401
(801) 392-9231
Olmrh@juno.com

Virginia

Mary Mother of the Church Abbey
12829 River Rd.
Richmond, VA 23233
(804) 784-3508
www.richmondmonks.org

Washington

The Priory Spirituality Center
500 College St. NE
Lacey, WA 98516
(360) 438-2595
spiritualityctr@stplacid.org

Wisconsin

St. Benedict's Abbey and Retreat Center
12605 244th
Benet Lake, WI 53102-0333
Toll free: (888) 482-1044
info@benetlake.org
www.osb.org/benlake

Saint Bede Retreat and Conference Center
P.O. Box 66
1190 Priory Rd.
Eau Claire, WI 54702-0066
(715) 834-8642
sisters@saintbede.org
www.saintbede.org

Monastery St. Benedict Center
4200 County Highway M
Middleton, WI 53562-2317
(608) 836-1631
Fax: (608) 831-9312
info@sbcenter.org
www.sbcenter.org

Glossary

In most cases the meanings given apply strictly to monastic life, specifically Benedictine, Cistercian, or Trappist life. Although references are generally made to monks, in most cases they also apply to nuns.

Abbey: An autonomous monastery of at least twelve monks, governed by an abbot or abbess, living according to the Rule of Saint Benedict. Benedict founded the first abbey at Monte Cassino near Rome in the sixth century.

Abbey of Gethsemani: The oldest Trappist monastery in the United States, founded in 1848 by a group of forty-four French monks from the Abbey of Melleray, near the Loire River in Brittany.

Abbot: The spiritual leader and chief administrator of a monastery, elected by professed monks to stand for Christ in their community. The term is derived from the Aramaic word *abba*, meaning "father." The term "abbess" is used for a female superior.

Abbot general: The elected superior of the nuns and monks of the Cistercian Order of the Strict Observance (Trappists).

Abbot's council: A committee of at least three monks who are constitutionally empowered to advise the abbot of a house and offer or withhold consent on certain matters.

Abbatial election: An abbot is chosen by majority vote, for either a six-year term, after which he may be reelected, or for an unrestricted term.

Anointing of the sick: One of the seven sacraments of the Catholic church, formerly called "extreme unction" or "last anointing." Bells call a Trappist monk to the bedside of a dying brother to pray with him when he is anointed.

Anthony of Egypt, St.: The early Coptic solitary who is considered the first Christian hermit. Called "the father of monasticism," he lived alone in radical simplicity in the Egyptian desert. Many third- and fourth-century Christians followed his example and joined him to lead lives of prayer and poverty in the wilderness.

Antiphon: A short verse of Scripture that is sung preceding and following a psalm. The "antiphonary" is a collection of such music.

Apostolate: A term used to describe the particular role of a group or individual in carrying out Christ's mission of redemption. Trappist monks are called to a contemplative apostolate, while parish priests, for example, are a part of the active apostolate.

Asceticism: The doctrine and practice of religious discipline with an emphasis on self-control and the fostering of virtue. Monastic life is rooted in Christian asceticism, which includes the practices of renunciation, self-denial, and penance.

Attention: In prayer, the focus on a particular object such as a breath, an image, or God's word in Scripture.

Augustine of Hippo, St.: The fourth-century bishop and author who converted to Christianity from paganism. His best-known work is *Confessions*, but he is also known for the monastic rule he wrote, which presently is followed by more than 150 religious communities.

***Aves* and *Paters*:** The simple prayers prayed in private by Cistercian lay brothers in the past, while choir monks chanted the liturgical hours in church. The term is Latin for the first words of the "Hail Mary" and the "Our Father" prayers.

Awareness: The act of being conscious of a thought or perception.

Balanced life: A Cistercian monastic value that emphasizes a life balanced between prayer and work.

Benedict of Nursia: The sixth-century founder of Western monasticism, author of the Rule of St. Benedict.

Benedict, St., The Rule of: The sixth-century monastic code that is today followed by men and women living in about twenty-seven communities around the world, not including lay associates, or oblates, who live by it outside of monasteries. The Rule combines spiritual doctrine with practical guidelines governing daily life in a monastery.

Benedictines: Those monasteries that follow the Rule of St. Benedict and belong to a confederation—not a centralized order—presided over by an abbot primate in Rome. There are currently more than twenty congregations of professed Benedictine monks in more than 250 monasteries, plus twenty-four federations of nuns (women in solemn vows) and thirty-four federations of sisters (women who take only simple vows). Benedictines perform a variety of work inside and outside the monastery, ranging from agriculture and hospitality to scholarship and parochial ministry.

Bernard of Clairvaux, St.: A dominant figure of the twelfth-century church, Bernard was a Cistercian abbot who developed a theology of reformed monasticism through his sermons, letters, and treatises.

Breviary: A book that contains the prayers, psalms, and readings of the Liturgy of the Hours.

Burial, Trappist: Trappist monks are buried without coffins in cemeteries marked by simple crosses of iron or wood.

Camaldolese: A monastic order that combines the Rule of Benedict with the hermit, or eremitical, life. The Congregation of Monk Hermits of Camaldoli was founded in the eleventh century as a Benedictine reform community.

Cantor: The monk who leads the monastic chant or song.

Capitulum: A short text of Scripture read during the liturgical hours of the day.

Carthusians: A monastic order that emphasizes the hermit, or eremitical, life. The cloistered monks and nuns live in hermitages, whereas the brothers and sisters have individual cells in the monastery. There is one Carthusian monastery in the United States, located in Vermont. Community is fostered by walks together in the countryside, with two each year lasting all day.

Celibacy: A monk's promise to forego marriage, and therefore sexual activity, as a sign of his dedication to God.

Cell: A monk's private room, the replacement for the dormitory cot that was the norm until the 1960s.

Cellarer: The monk who organizes the work of a Trappist monastery and is responsible for the abbey's material needs. Similar to a business manager, a cellarer is the only monk, apart from the abbot, who can act in the name of the monastery when incurring expenses and in legal matters.

Cenobite: A monk who lives communally, as opposed to a hermit.

Centering prayer: A form of prayer, also called contemplation, that is based on the prayer of the Desert Fathers. The Cistercian form, which uses a sacred word to help the meditator attend only to God and the Holy Spirit's inspirations, has been popularized by the American Trappists Thomas Keating and Basil Pennington.

Chaplain: A monk assigned as a spiritual director to a convent of Trappistine nuns. He is not involved in governing the community but says its daily Mass. Also, a monk who performs these duties for a retreat house.

Chapter: A meeting of all the monks in a house to conduct community business in a designated chapter room. The name comes from the monastic practice of assembling daily to hear a chapter of the Rule read aloud. Chapters can be local, provincial, or general, the last representing an entire monastic order. They encourage and nurture the active involvement of members of a community.

Chapter of Faults: A meeting where monks accused ("proclaimed") themselves or one another of violations of the community's customs or rules. The superior decided upon suitable penances. The practice ended in the 1960s.

Chapter Room: The room in a monastery where chapter meetings are held.

Charter of Charity: Charta caritatis, the eleventh-century constitution that created the Cistercian order and bound all its abbots to come to Citeaux, France, annually for a General Chapter. It also called for all houses to observe common guidelines and set up a system of visitation that respected the autonomy of each house while assuring its fidelity to the order.

Charterhouse: The traditional name for a monastery of Carthusian monks.

Choir: Monks are said to be seated "in choir" when they are assembled in two groups facing each other across the central aisle of an abbey church during a liturgical hour.

Choir monk: Prior to the 1960s, a Trappist who entered a monastery with the intention of pursuing studies to become a priest. He lived in separate quarters, received different training, and performed a different kind of work than his monastic counterpart, the lay brother. Today, the training and lifestyle of the two vocations have merged.

Church: The heart of the monastery, where the community gathers for daily Mass and all liturgical hours. Cistercian churches are designed in the form of a cross.

Cistercian Lay Contemplatives (CLC): Men and women who form an association to support individual and group efforts to live a contemplative spirituality based on Cistercian values and practices. Founded in the United States in the 1980s, the group abides by a document called "Plan of Life," a guide to integrating monastic practice into ordinary life.

Cistercian Order of the Strict Observance (OCSO): Also known as the Order of Reformed Cistercians (OCR), nicknamed "Trappists," after the strict reforms initiated by Armand-Jean de Rance at the Monastery of La Trappe in France. It is distinct from the Order of Common Observance (OCO) of the Cistercians, who follow a more active apostolate and a less ascetic lifestyle.

Cloister: The areas of a monastery reserved exclusively for the monks who live there. The term also refers to a covered walkway, usually quadrangular in shape and open to the weather, that surrounds a garden in a monastery.

Compline: The final liturgical office of the day, the night prayer of the monks.

Constitutions and Statutes of the Cistercian Order of the Strict Observance: The body of laws, created and revised by the General Chapter, that governs Trappist monks and nuns.

Contemplation: A form of wordless prayer that is the ultimate stage of the process monks call *lectio divina*. It is considered a gift from God, not a technique that can be willed or mastered. See centering prayer.

Contemplative Outreach: A spiritual network of individuals and small communities whose primary focus is to encourage the practice of the Christian contemplative tradition. It sponsors centering-prayer workshops through local chapters across the country.

Contemplatives: A term broadly used to describe those religious who are devoted to a simple life of prayer and work rather than an "active" apostolate like teaching, nursing, or counseling.

Conventual Mass: The daily Mass celebrated with the monastic community in attendance.

Conversion: From the Latin *convertere,* meaning "to turn around," this term refers to the monk's commitment to reject his former life and its complacency and to be open to the will of God through the practices of his community.

Cowl: A unique, white hooded cloak worn over the habit and given at solemn profession.

Crozier: A staff with a crook at the top, a symbol of the pastoral office of an abbot.

Decree of Unification: A 1965 Trappist reform that combined the formerly distinct vocations of lay brother and choir monk.

Desert Fathers and Mothers: The spiritual leaders of the Christian monastic movement of the early church who lived in Egypt and Palestine. They included Anthony of Egypt, Abba Moses, and Amma Sarah. Their wisdom has been preserved in *Sayings of the Elders,* a collection of stories and proverbs.

Dom: An honorific used for a Trappist abbot. An abbreviation of the Latin word, *dominus* ("master"), the term is applied to any professed monk by Benedictines and some other monastic orders.

Enclosure: In a monastery, the border between monastic areas (the cloister) and areas open to visitors. It is traditionally a high wall with locked gates or doors.

Eremitical: Related to the hermit life.

Eucharist: Derived from the Greek word for "thanksgiving," the Eucharist is the sacramental celebration of the Paschal Mystery (Christ's dying and rising for humankind).

Exclaustration: Official permission granted to a monk to leave his monastery.

Father immediate: The abbot of a Trappist monastery who is appointed to oversee daughter houses of monks and nuns founded from a particular monastery.

Feast days: Days in the church calendar set aside to commemorate significant events in the life of Christ, the saints, or the Christian people. In general, feast days rank in significance between "solemnities," such as Easter, and "memorials," the designation for most saints' days.

Filiation: A system of monastic governance, based on mother houses and daughter houses, that was an early Cistercian reform of the Benedictines. The point was to give autonomy to a house while assuring its fidelity to the order.

Garth: An open courtyard or garden surrounded by the cloister; also called a *préau*.

General Chapter of Abbots: The meeting every three years of all abbots and abbesses of Cistercian monasteries.

Gethsemani: A garden outside Jerusalem, mentioned by name in the Gospels of Matthew and Mark as the site of the agony and arrest of Jesus. It is sometimes used as a metaphor for a place or occasion of great spiritual or mental suffering. Gethsemani Abbey took its name from the Sisters of Loretto at the Foot of the Cross, who owned the land before selling it to the French Trappists in 1848.

Gethsemani Encounter: An international meeting of Buddhist and Catholic monks from around the world, including the Dalai Lama, that took place at Gethsemani in 1996.

Grand Silence: A period of silence, at some monasteries, from compline until the end of Mass the next morning.

Gregorian chant: The plainchant of the Catholic church, traditionally sung by monks without musical accompaniment.

Habit: A garment worn by monastics. The Cistercian habit includes a white tunic, a black scapular (hooded apron), a leather belt, and a white hooded garment known as a cowl. Monks who have not yet made solemn vows wear a simple white cloak rather than a cowl.

Hermit: A monk dedicated to a life of absolute solitude for the sake of prayer, penance, recollection, and closer union with God. The best-known hermit of the early Church was Anthony of Egypt.

Holy water: Water that is blessed. A reminder of the holy waters of baptism, it is placed in fonts and in containers at the doorways of Catholic churches, where people dip into it and make the sign of the cross. At Trappist monasteries, the abbot sprinkles holy water on monks and visitors as a night blessing at the end of compline.

Hours: Also known as *Opus Dei,* meaning "Work of God," the hours are obligatory times of daily liturgical prayer in Benedictine monasteries. Also known as the Liturgy of the Hours, it includes vigils, lauds, terce, sext, none, vespers, and compline.

Incense: The aromatic gums of resinous trees burned on coals in a brazier (stationary metal container) or in portable containers called thuribles, which are censers suspended from a short chain and swung gently to create smoke. Incense is used during Catholic processions and to honor sacred objects such as the altar. The person who holds the thurible in a procession is the thurifer.

Infirmary: The rooms or buildings set aside in a monastery for monks who are sick or who need special care due to advanced age or disability.

John of the Cross, St.: The Catholic mystic and saint of the Carmelite order who wrote treatises on contemplation, including *The Dark Night of the Soul,* offering insight into an individual's movement toward union with God, and much consulted by monastics.

Lauds: The official morning prayer of a monastic community.

Laura: Originally a community of semireclusive monks under the direction of one spiritual father or superior. In a laura, monks live as solitaries in scattered cells, usually in a remote or desert area within walking distance of a common monastic building. Today, laura is used also to mean any large Eastern Orthodox monastery.

Lavabo: A ceremony in the Mass in which the priest washes his hands reciting part of Psalm 25, beginning with the word *lavabo,* meaning "I shall wash." It symbolizes the purification of body and soul in preparation for the most sacred and essential part of the Mass.

Lay brother: A monk who fully participates in membership of a community but is not an ordained priest. Trappist lay brothers traditionally devoted more time to manual labor than the choir monks and were exempt from attending the liturgical hours. Rather, they prayed their prayers as a group in private. Also known as *conversi.*

Lay work force: Hired employees of a Trappist monastery who are not members of the community. Lay workers are a growing need as the average size of communities dwindles and ages.

Lectio divina: Latin for "sacred reading," this ancient monastic practice of reading Scripture and other texts is designed to lead a monk toward union with God. Lectio has four stages: reading, meditating, prayer, and contemplation. It is central to Trappist contemplative life.

Lent: A period of forty days (not counting Sundays) of fasting and prayer before Easter.

Little Hours: The three brief midday liturgical hours of terce, sext, and none.

Liturgy: The system of public prayers and sacred texts and ceremonies established by the church as its official vehicle of worship.

Mass: The traditional name for the Eucharist, the celebration of the death and resurrection of Christ, the central mystery of the Catholic faith. It is a service of Scripture readings, psalms, prayer, and preaching, followed by Communion. Mass is said daily in Trappist monasteries.

Master of Novices: The monk who supervises the formation, or training, of newcomers to the community.

Matins: Another name for vigils.

Meditation: A process of mental prayer or silent listening aimed at bringing one closer to union with God through concentration and awareness. It is one stage of *lectio divina,* as practiced by Trappists and others.

Merton, Thomas: A prolific essayist, diarist, poet, social critic, peace activist, teacher, and hermit of the Abbey of Gethsemani, where he was known as Father Louis. Arguably the best-known Christian monk of modern times, he died in Thailand in 1968 while attending a monastic conference in Bangkok.

Monastery: In Catholic terminology, the dwelling place of monks, nuns, or other religious living a communal life under a common rule. Monasteries are named by their superiors' rank (abbey or priory) or the work done there (mission or house of studies.)

Monk: Derived from the Latin word *monachus,* a transliteration of the Greek for "one who lives alone," the term today refers to any member of a religious community of men who take vows and live under a monastic rule. In the medieval church, it referred only to Benedictines, Cistercians, and Carthusians.

None: The midafternoon liturgical office, said at 2:15 PM at Gethsemani.

Novice: An aspirant to the monastic life who lives in community but has not yet taken vows.

Novitiate: The part of a monastery assigned to the novices as a place of training and residence.

Nun: A woman who takes solemn vows in a religious order, in contrast to a "sister," who takes simple vows.

Obedience: A monk's surrender of his personal will in order to be free to do God's will; a vow taken by Benedictines and Trappists.

Oblates: Lay men and women who are affiliated with a Benedictine monastery and share a spiritual union and human friendship with the community. The term is derived from the Latin word *oblatus,* which indicates someone who is dedicated to something. A Benedictine oblate receives a small version of a scapular, such as monks wear, in a ceremony known as investiture.

Office: The ordinary term for the daily round of liturgical prayers that begins with vigils and ends with compline.

Order: A religious society established under the authority of the pope, in which members are bound by solemn vows. It differs from a "congregation," whose members take simple vows and operate with diocesan, but not papal, approval.

Pluralism: A value of Cistercian life that was reaffirmed by the Catholic church reforms of the 1960s and remains an important issue today. Pluralism not only affirms individual differences among monks in a community, but also recognizes cultural differences between developing-nation communities and those in Western countries.

Postulant: One who has applied for entry into an order and undergoes a brief trial period before being admitted as a novice.

Poverty: The monastic value that requires a monk to give up all his material goods, but even more important, to surrender himself wholly to God and his community. Trusting that God will provide for him through his brothers, the monk can then focus on a simple life of work and prayer for the good of others.

Prayer: An essential element of monastic life, prayer is the act of entering into conscious, loving communion with God. Ideally, prayer is integrated into every activity a monk pursues, not just the public worship he is called to at appointed times of the day.

Préau: The garden inside the enclosed cloister of a monastery; also called a *garth*.

Prior: The monk who is second-in-command at an abbey, or is the superior of a priory, which is a Trappist monastery that has not yet reached the independent status of an abbey. A Trappist prior assumes authority in the abbot's absence.

Professed: Monks who have taken vows. In Trappist communities, they include the "simple professed" and the "solemn professed."

Psalms: The 150 prayers from the Bible's Book of Psalms that are the heart of a Trappist monastery's daily liturgy of hours. Trappists complete the full cycle of psalms every two weeks. The Psalter is the liturgical book from which a monk chants in church.

Refectory: The monastic dining room. This is where all meals are taken and where books are read aloud during the main meal of the Trappist day.

Reforms: In the Trappist tradition, a recurring cycle of returning to more primitive and simple lifestyles following periods of relaxation of monastic rules. The Cistercian Order was a reform of eleventh-century Benedictine life, and the Trappist, or Strict Observance, reform was an effort to restore a more austere asceticism to seventeenth-century Cistercian monasticism. The last round of major reforms came in the 1960s, in the wake of across-the-board changes in Catholic spiritual and religious practice.

Retreat: A time of personal withdrawal, intended as a way of refreshing one's spiritual life through prayer, meditation, and study. The Trappist Constitutions call for each monk to have a week-long personal retreat annually, and for each house to have a community retreat once a year.

Retreat house: A portion of a monastery set aside for overnight visitors seeking spiritual revival, supervised by a monk known as the guestmaster. Based on Christ's admonition to "welcome the stranger," hospitality is a Benedictine tradition. Retreat houses vary in size, but most offer undirected retreats in a secluded, usually rural, setting. It is customary for an aspirant to a Trappist monastery to spend time there first on retreat.

Sacristy: A room located to one side of the sanctuary of a Catholic church where priests and others dress and prepare for liturgical ceremonies.

Salve Regina: The opening Latin words of the hymn "Hail, Holy Queen," which is sung or recited after some liturgical hours. At Gethsemani, it is traditionally sung at the end of compline as a final prayer of the day.

Sanctuary: The space in a church immediately surrounding the altar.

Scapular: A narrow cloak or apron that hangs down the front and back of the one who wears it; a traditional garment in religious orders. Trappists receive a black scapular at solemn profession.

Schola: A group of monks within the monastic choir that sings as a separate group during liturgical hours or other church services.

Scriptorium: The monastic reading room where newspapers and periodicals are available for monks to read. Before dormitories were replaced by private cells, each monk had a desk in the scriptorium where he conducted his studies.

Seclusion: A traditional element of Cistercian monastic life, reflected in the remote geographical setting of abbeys and the emphasis on silence and contemplation.

Secular: Anything or anyone not associated with religious communities.

Sext: The midday liturgical office, celebrated at 12:15 PM at Gethsemani.

Sign language: A nonverbal form of communication that Trappists used, when necessary, during earlier times of strict silence.

Silence: A principal monastic value of the Trappists. No longer practiced as a rigid rule, silence is viewed as a means of fostering solitude and opening the mind to the inspiration of God.

Skete: A small monastic settlement with a few monks living under the authority of an elder.

Spiritual Directory: The official book of formation for the Cistercian Order.

Stability: A Trappist monk's vow to spend the remainder of his life in the community of his profession, forcing him to confront his problems where he is rather than trying to escape or evade them by moving elsewhere.

Terce: The morning liturgical office, celebrated at 7:30 AM at Gethsemani.

Trappist: The common name for the Order of Cistercians of the Strict Observance (OCSO). The name is derived from the French Abbey of La Trappe, the site of an austere Cistercian reform in the seventeenth century. The Trappist name is used to distinguish the order from the Order of Cistercians of the Common Observance (OCO), which lives a less ascetic communal life and is a more active order.

Trappistines: Trappist nuns. An order of female monastics who trace their origins to the founding of a cloister for women at Tart, near Citeaux, France, soon after the Cistercian order began there. Like the Trappists, the Trappistines represent a reform movement that was initiated at the Abbey of La Trappe in France.

Union: Also known as "divine union," this term applies to the experience of uniting all thinking and feeling in God.

Vespers: The evening prayer of the monastic community, one of the major liturgical hours. At Gethsemani, it arrives at 5:30 PM, just before the evening meal.

Vigils: The first of the liturgical hours, it is the opening prayer of the monk's day, full of hope and thanksgiving. At Gethsemani, it begins at 3:15 AM.

Visitation: The official annual visit to a Trappist monastery by the abbot of its mother house, who is also known as the father immediate. The visitor meets privately with each community member, and then executes written recommendations.

Vows: Promises to God made by members of religious communities. Trappists first take temporary "simple" vows, followed by permanent "solemn" vows, of stability, obedience, and conversion of manners, which include poverty and chastity.

About SKYLIGHT PATHS Publishing

SkyLight Paths Publishing is creating a place where people of different spiritual traditions come together for challenge and inspiration, a place where we can help each other understand the mystery that lies at the heart of our existence.

Through spirituality, our religious beliefs are increasingly becoming a part of our lives—rather than *apart* from our lives. While many of us may be more interested than ever in spiritual growth, we may be less firmly planted in traditional religion. Yet, we do want to deepen our relationship to the sacred, to learn from our own as well as from other faith traditions, and to practice in new ways.

SkyLight Paths sees both believers and seekers as a community that increasingly transcends traditional boundaries of religion and denomination—people wanting to learn from each other, *walking together, finding the way.*

We at SkyLight Paths take great care to produce beautiful books that present meaningful spiritual content in a form that reflects the art of making high quality books. Therefore, we want to acknowledge those who contributed to the production of this book.

PRODUCTION
Marian B. Wallace & Bridgett Taylor

EDITORIAL
David O'Neal & Emily Wichland

COVER DESIGN
Bronwen Battaglia, Scituate, Massachusetts

TEXT DESIGN
Chelsea Cloeter, Scotia, New York

PRINTING AND BINDING
Lake Book, Melrose Park, Illinois

Other Interesting Books—Spirituality

Show Me Your Way
The Complete Guide to Exploring Interfaith Spiritual Direction
by *Howard A. Addison*

An ancient spiritual practice—reimagined for the modern seeker. Introduces people of all faiths—even those with no particular religious involvement—to the concept and practice of spiritual direction and, for the first time, to the dynamics of *interfaith* spiritual direction.
5½ x 8½, 240 pp, Quality PB, ISBN 1-893361-41-1 **$16.95**; HC, ISBN 1-893361-12-8 **$21.95**

Waking Up: *A Week Inside a Zen Monastery*
by *Jack Maguire*; Foreword by *John Daido Loori, Roshi*

An essential guide to what it's like to spend a week inside a Zen Buddhist monastery.
6 x 9, 224 pp, b/w photographs, HC, ISBN 1-893361-13-6 **$21.95**

  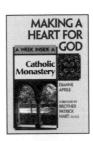 

Making a Heart for God: *A Week Inside a Catholic Monastery*
by *Dianne Aprile*; Foreword by *Brother Patrick Hart*, O.C.S.O.

This essential guide to experiencing life in a Catholic monastery takes us to the Abbey of Gethsemani—the Trappist monastery in Kentucky that was home to author Thomas Merton—to explore the details. "More balanced and informative than the popular *The Cloister Walk* by Kathleen Norris." —*Choice: Current Reviews for Academic Libraries*
6 x 9, 224 pp, b/w photographs, Quality PB, ISBN 1-893361-49-7 **$16.95**;
HC, ISBN 1-893361-14-4 **$21.95**

Come and Sit: *A Week Inside Meditation Centers*
by *Marcia Z. Nelson*; Foreword by *Wayne Teasdale*

The insider's guide to meditation in a variety of different spiritual traditions. Traveling through Buddhist, Hindu, Christian, Jewish, and Sufi traditions, this essential guide takes the reader to different meditation centers to meet the teachers and students and learn about the practices, demystifying the meditation experience for people of all levels.
6 x 9, 224 pp, b/w photographs, Quality PB Original, ISBN 1-893361-35-7 **$16.95**

Or phone, fax, mail or e-mail to: SKYLIGHT PATHS Publishing
Sunset Farm Offices, Route 4 • P.O. Box 237 • Woodstock, Vermont 05091
Tel: (802) 457-4000   Fax: (802) 457-4004   www.skylightpaths.com
Credit card orders: (800) 962-4544 (9AM–5PM ET Monday–Friday)
Generous discounts on quantity orders. Satisfaction guaranteed. Prices subject to change.

Spirituality

Who Is My God?
An Innovative Guide to Finding Your Spiritual Identity
Created by *the Editors at SkyLight Paths*

Spiritual Type™ + Tradition Indicator = Spiritual Identity

Your Spiritual Identity is an undeniable part of who you are—whether you've thought much about it or not. This dynamic resource provides a helpful framework to begin or deepen your spiritual growth. Start by taking the unique Spiritual Identity Self-Test™; tabulate your results; then explore one, two or more of twenty-eight faiths/spiritual paths followed in America today. "An innovative and entertaining way to think—and rethink—about your own spiritual path, or perhaps even to find one." —Dan Wakefield, author of *How Do We Know When It's God?*
6 x 9, 160 pp, Quality PB Original, ISBN 1-893361-08-X **$15.95**

Spiritual Manifestos: *Visions for Renewed Religious Life in America from Young Spiritual Leaders of Many Faiths*
Edited by *Niles Elliot Goldstein*; Preface by *Martin E. Marty*

Discover the reasons why so many people have kept organized religion at arm's length.

Here, ten young spiritual leaders, most in their mid-thirties, representing the spectrum of religious traditions—Protestant, Catholic, Jewish, Buddhist, Unitarian Universalist—present the innovative ways they are transforming our spiritual communities and our lives. "These ten articulate young spiritual leaders engender hope for the vitality of 21st-century religion." —Forrest Church, Minister of All Souls Church in New York City
6 x 9, 256 pp, HC, ISBN 1-893361-09-8 **$21.95**

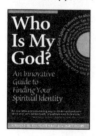 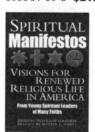  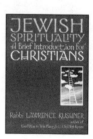

Jewish Spirituality: *A Brief Introduction for Christians*
by *Lawrence Kushner*

Lawrence Kushner, whose award-winning books have brought Jewish spirituality to life for countless readers of all faiths and backgrounds, tailors his unique style to address Christian's questions, revealing the essence of Judaism in a way that people whose own tradition traces its roots to Judaism can understand and enjoy. Offers Christian readers tools to strengthen their own faith.
5½ x 8½, 112 pp, Quality PB Original, ISBN 1-58023-150-0 **$12.95** A JEWISH LIGHTS Book

The Geography of Faith
Underground Conversations on Religious, Political, and Social Change
by *Robert Coles* and *Daniel Berrigan*; Updated foreword and afterword by the authors

A classic of faith-based activism—updated for a new generation.

Listen in on the conversations between these two great teachers—one a renegade priest wanted by the FBI for his protests against the Vietnam war, the other a future Pulitzer Prize-winning journalist—as they struggle with what it means to put your faith to the test. Discover how their story of challenging the status quo during a time of great political, religious, and social change is just as applicable to our lives today. 6 x 9, 208 pp, Quality PB, ISBN 1-893361-40-3 **$16.95**

Spirituality

Three Gates to Meditation Practice
A Personal Journey into Sufism, Buddhism, and Judaism
by *David A. Cooper*

Shows us how practicing within more than one spiritual tradition can lead us to our true home.

Here are over fifteen years from the journey of "post-denominational rabbi" David A. Cooper, author of *God Is a Verb*, and his wife, Shoshana—years in which the Coopers explored a rich variety of practices, from chanting Sufi *dhikr* to Buddhist Vipassanā meditation, to the study of kabbalah and esoteric Judaism. Their experience demonstrates that the spiritual path is really completely within our reach, whoever we are, whatever we do—as long as we are willing to practice it. 5½ x 8½, 240 pp, Quality PB, ISBN 1-893361-22-5 **$16.95**

Praying with Our Hands: *Twenty-One Practices of Embodied Prayer from the World's Spiritual Traditions*
by *Jon M. Sweeney*; Photographs by *Jennifer J. Wilson*;
Foreword by *Mother Tessa Bielecki*; Afterword by *Taitetsu Unno, Ph.D.*

A spiritual guidebook for bringing prayer into our bodies.

What gives our prayers meaning? How can we carry a prayerful spirit throughout our everyday lives? This inspiring book of reflections and accompanying photographs shows us twenty-one simple ways of using our hands to speak to God, to enrich our devotion and ritual. All express the various approaches of the world's religious traditions to bringing the body into worship. Spiritual traditions represented include Anglican, Sufi, Zen, Roman Catholic, Yoga, Shaker, Hindu, Jewish, Pentecostal, Eastern Orthodox, and many others.
8 x 8, 96 pp, 22 duotone photographs, Quality PB Original, ISBN 1-893361-16-0 **$16.95**

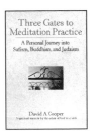  

Labyrinths from the Outside In
Walking to Spiritual Insight—a Beginner's Guide
by *Donna Schaper* & *Carole Ann Camp*

The user-friendly, interfaith guide to making and using labyrinths—for meditation, prayer, and celebration.

Labyrinth walking is a spiritual exercise *anyone* can do. And it's rare among such practices in that it can be done by people together, regardless of their religious backgrounds or lack thereof. This accessible guide unlocks the mysteries of the labyrinth for all of us, providing ideas for using the labyrinth walk for prayer, meditation, and celebrations to mark the most important moments in life. Includes instructions for making a labyrinth of your own and finding one in your area.
6 x 9, 208 pp, b/w illus. and photographs, Quality PB Original, ISBN 1-893361-18-7 **$16.95**

Spirituality

Honey from the Rock
An Introduction to Jewish Mysticism
by *Lawrence Kushner*

An insightful and absorbing introduction to the ten gates of Jewish mysticism and how it applies to daily life. "The easiest introduction to Jewish mysticism you can read."
6 x 9, 176 pp, Quality PB, ISBN 1-58023-073-3 **$15.95**

Eyes Remade for Wonder
The Way of Jewish Mysticism and Sacred Living
A Lawrence Kushner Reader

Intro. by *Thomas Moore*, author of *Care of the Soul*

Whether you are new to Kushner or a devoted fan, you'll find inspiration here. With samplings from each of Kushner's works, and a generous amount of new material, this book is to be read and reread, each time discovering deeper layers of meaning in our lives.
6 x 9, 240 pp, Quality PB, ISBN 1-58023-042-3 **$16.95**; HC, ISBN 1-58023-014-8 **$23.95**

Invisible Lines of Connection
Sacred Stories of the Ordinary
by *Lawrence Kushner*   AWARD WINNER!

Through his everyday encounters with family, friends, colleagues and strangers, Kushner takes us deeply into our lives, finding flashes of spiritual insight in the process.
5½ x 8½, 160 pp, Quality PB, ISBN 1-879045-98-2 **$15.95**; HC, ISBN 1-879045-52-4 **$21.95**

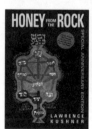    

Finding Joy
A Practical Spiritual Guide to Happiness
by *Dannel I. Schwartz* with *Mark Hass*   AWARD WINNER!

Explains how to find joy through a time honored, creative—and surprisingly practical—approach based on the teachings of Jewish mysticism and Kabbalah.
6 x 9, 192 pp, Quality PB, ISBN 1-58023-009-1 **$14.95**; HC, ISBN 1-879045-53-2 **$19.95**

Ancient Secrets
Using the Stories of the Bible to Improve Our Everyday Lives
by *Rabbi Levi Meier, Ph.D.*   AWARD WINNER!

Drawing on a broad range of wisdom writings, distinguished rabbi and psychologist Levi Meier takes a thoughtful, wise and fresh approach to showing us how to apply the stories of the Bible to our everyday lives.
5½ x 8½, 288 pp, Quality PB, ISBN 1-58023-064-4 **$16.95**

Spirituality

One God Clapping: *The Spiritual Path of a Zen Rabbi*
by *Alan Lew* with *Sherril Jaffe*

Firsthand account of a spiritual journey from Zen Buddhist practitioner to rabbi.

A fascinating personal story of a Jewish meditation expert's roundabout spiritual journey from Zen Buddhist practitioner to rabbi. An insightful source of inspiration for each of us who is on the journey to find God in today's multi-faceted spiritual world.
5½ x 8½, 336 pp, Quality PB, ISBN 1-58023-115-2 **$16.95**

The Way of a Pilgrim: *Annotated & Explained*
Translation & annotation by *Gleb Pokrovsky;*
Foreword by *Andrew Harvey,* SkyLight Illuminations series editor

The classic of Russian spirituality—now with facing-page commentary that illuminates and explains the text.

This delightful account is the story of one man who sets out to learn the prayer of the heart—also known as the "Jesus prayer"—and how the practice transforms his existence. This SkyLight Illuminations edition guides you through an abridged version of the text with facing-page annotations explaining the names, terms and references.
5½ x 8½, 160 pp, Quality PB, ISBN 1-893361-31-4 **$14.95**

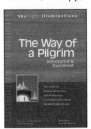   

Bhagavad Gita: *Annotated & Explained*
Translation by *Shri Purohit Swami;* Annotation by *Kendra Crossen Burroughs;*
Foreword by *Andrew Harvey,* SkyLight Illuminations series editor

"The very best Gita for first-time readers." —Ken Wilber

Millions of people turn daily to India's most beloved holy book, whose universal appeal has made it popular with non-Hindus and Hindus alike. This SkyLight Illuminations edition of the Gita introduces readers to the characters; explains references and philosophical terms; shares the interpretations of famous spiritual leaders and scholars; and more.
5½ x 8½, 208 pp, Quality PB, ISBN 1-893361-28-4 **$15.95**

The New Millennium Spiritual Journey
Change Your Life—Develop Your Spiritual Priorities with Help from Today's Most Inspiring Spiritual Teachers
Created by *the Editors at SkyLight Paths*

A life-changing resource for reimagining your spiritual life.

Set your own course of reflection and spiritual transformation with the help of self-tests, spirituality exercises, sacred texts from many traditions, time capsule pages, and helpful suggestions from more than 20 spiritual teachers, including Karen Armstrong, Sylvia Boorstein and Dr. Andrew Weil. 7 x 9, 144 pp, Quality PB Original, ISBN 1-893361-05-5 **$16.95**

Spirituality

Inspired Lives: *Exploring the Role of Faith and Spirituality in the Lives of Extraordinary People*

by *Joanna Laufer* & *Kenneth S. Lewis*

Contributors include *Ang Lee, Wynton Marsalis, Kathleen Norris,* and many more

How faith transforms the lives and work of the creative and innovative people in our world.

In this moving book, soul-searching conversations unearth the importance of spirituality and personal faith for more than forty artists and innovators who have made a real difference in our world through their work. 6 x 9, 256 pp, Quality PB, ISBN 1-893361-33-0 **$16.95**

Women Pray

Voices through the Ages, from Many Faiths, Cultures, and Traditions

Edited and with introductions by *Monica Furlong*

Many ways—new and old—to communicate with the Divine.

Celebrates the rich variety of ways women from many faiths, cultures, and traditions have called out to the Divine. Includes prayers by Sappho, Denise Levertov, Mirabai, Rabi'a the Mystic, Alice Walker, and many others. "An invitation to enter into the personal and passionate felt presence of the divine with another woman." —*Sylvia Boorstein*

5 x 7¼, 256 pp, Deluxe HC with ribbon marker, ISBN 1-893361-25-X **$19.95**

  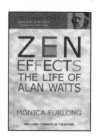 

Zen Effects: *The Life of Alan Watts*

by *Monica Furlong*

The first and only full-length biography of one of the most charismatic spiritual leaders of the twentieth century—now back in print!

Through his widely popular books and lectures, Alan Watts (1915–1973) did more to introduce Eastern philosophy and religion to Western minds than any figure before or since. Here is the only biography of this charismatic figure, who served as Zen teacher, Anglican priest, lecturer, academic, entertainer, a leader of the San Francisco renaissance, and author of more than 30 books, including *The Way of Zen, Psychotherapy East and West* and *The Spirit of Zen.*
6 x 9, 264 pp, Quality PB, ISBN 1-893361-32-2 **$16.95**

Simone Weil: *A Modern Pilgrimage*

by *Robert Coles*

The extraordinary life of the spiritual philosopher who's been called both saint and madwoman.

The French writer and philosopher Simone Weil (1906–1943) devoted her life to a search for God—while avoiding membership in organized religion. Robert Coles' intriguing study of Weil details her short, eventful life, and is an insightful portrait of the beloved and controversial thinker whose life and writings influenced many (from T.S. Eliot to Adrienne Rich to Albert Camus), and continue to inspire seekers everywhere. 6 x 9, 208 pp, Quality PB, ISBN 1-893361-34-9 **$16.95**

Spirituality

A Heart of Stillness
A Complete Guide to Learning the Art of Meditation
by *David A. Cooper*

The only complete, nonsectarian guide to meditation, from one of our most respected spiritual teachers.

Experience what mystics have experienced for thousands of years. *A Heart of Stillness* helps you acquire on your own, with minimal guidance, the skills of various styles of meditation. Draws upon the wisdom teachings of Christianity, Judaism, Buddhism, Hinduism, and Islam as it teaches you the processes of purification, concentration, and mastery in detail.
5½ x 8½, 272 pp, Quality PB, ISBN 1-893361-03-9 **$16.95**

Silence, Simplicity & Solitude
A Complete Guide to Spiritual Retreat at Home
by *David A. Cooper*

The classic personal spiritual retreat guide that enables readers to create their own self-guided spiritual retreat at home.

Award-winning author David Cooper traces personal mystical retreat in all of the world's major traditions, describing the varieties of spiritual practices for modern spiritual seekers. Cooper shares the techniques and practices that encompass the personal spiritual retreat experience, allowing readers to enhance their meditation practices and create an effective, self-guided spiritual retreat in their own homes—without the instruction of a meditation teacher. 5½ x 8½, 336 pp, Quality PB, ISBN 1-893361-04-7 **$16.95**

  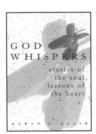 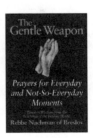 

God Whispers: *Stories of the Soul, Lessons of the Heart*
by Rabbi Karyn D. Kedar 6 x 9, 176 pp, Quality PB, ISBN 1-58023-088-1 **$15.95**

The Empty Chair: *Finding Hope and Joy—*
Timeless Wisdom from a Hasidic Master, Rebbe Nachman of Breslov AWARD WINNER!
Adapted by Moshe Mykoff and the Breslov Research Institute
4 x 6, 128 pp, Deluxe PB, 2-color text, ISBN 1-879045-67-2 **$9.95**

The Gentle Weapon: *Prayers for Everyday and Not-So-Everyday Moments*
Adapted from the Wisdom of Rebbe Nachman of Breslov by Moshe Mykoff and
S. C. Mizrahi, with the Breslov Research Institute
4 x 6, 144 pp, Deluxe PB, 2-color text, ISBN 1-58023-022-9 **$9.95**

Children's Spirituality

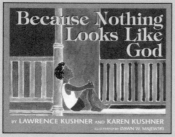

Because Nothing Looks Like God

by *Lawrence and Karen Kushner*

Full-color illus. by
Dawn W. Majewski

For ages 4 & up

MULTICULTURAL, NONDENOMINATIONAL,
NONSECTARIAN

Real-life examples of happiness and sadness—from goodnight stories, to the hope and fear felt the first time at bat, to the closing moments of life—introduce children to the possibilities of spiritual life. A vibrant way for children—and their adults—to explore what, where, and how God is in our lives.

11 x 8½, 32 pp, HC, Full-color illus., ISBN 1-58023-092-X **$16.95**

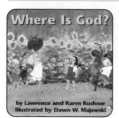   

Where Is God? (A Board Book)

For ages 0–4

by *Lawrence and Karen Kushner*; Full-color illus. by *Dawn W. Majewski*

A gentle way for young children to explore how God is with us every day, in every way. Abridged from *Because Nothing Looks Like God* by Lawrence and Karen Kushner and specially adapted to board book format to delight and inspire young readers.

5 x 5, 24 pp, Board, Full-color illus., ISBN 1-893361-17-9 **$7.95**

What Does God Look Like? (A Board Book)

For ages 0–4

by *Lawrence and Karen Kushner*; Full-color illus. by *Dawn W. Majewski*

A simple way for young children to explore the ways that we "see" God. Abridged from *Because Nothing Looks Like God* by Lawrence and Karen Kushner and specially adapted to board book format to delight and inspire young readers.

5 x 5, 24 pp, Board, Full-color illus., ISBN 1-893361-23-3 **$7.95**

How Does God Make Things Happen? (A Board Book)

For ages 0–4

by *Lawrence and Karen Kushner*; Full-color illus. by *Dawn W. Majewski*

A charming invitation for young children to explore how God makes things happen in our world. Abridged from *Because Nothing Looks Like God* by Lawrence and Karen Kushner and specially adapted to board book format to delight and inspire young readers.

5 x 5, 24 pp, Board, Full-color illus., ISBN 1-893361-24-1 **$7.95**

What Is God's Name? (A Board Book)

For ages 0–4

by *Sandy Eisenberg Sasso*; Full-color illus. by *Phoebe Stone*

Everyone and everything in the world has a name. What is God's name? Abridged from the award-winning *In God's Name* by Sandy Eisenberg Sasso and specially adapted to board book format to delight and inspire young readers.

5 x 5, 24 pp, Board, Full-color illus., ISBN 1-893361-10-1 **$7.95**

Children's Spirituality

Becoming Me: *A Story of Creation*
by *Martin Boroson*

For ages
4 & up

Full-color illus. by *Christopher Gilvan-Cartwright*

Told in the personal "voice" of the Creator, here is a story about creation and relationship that is about each one of us. In simple words and with radiant illustrations, the Creator tells an intimate story about love, about friendship and playing, about our world—and about ourselves. And with each turn of the page, we're reminded that we just might be closer to our Creator than we think!

8 x 10, 32 pp, Full-color illus., HC, ISBN 1-893361-11-X **$16.95**

A Prayer for the Earth
The Story of Naamah, Noah's Wife
by *Sandy Eisenberg Sasso*
Full-color illus. by *Bethanne Andersen*

For ages
4 & up

This new story, based on an ancient text, opens readers' religious imaginations to new ideas about the well-known story of the Flood. When God tells Noah to bring the animals of the world onto the ark, God also calls on Naamah, Noah's wife, to save each plant on Earth. "A lovely tale. . . . Children of all ages should be drawn to this parable for our times." —Tomie de Paola, artist/author of books for children
9 x 12, 32 pp, HC, Full-color illus., ISBN 1-879045-60-5 **$16.95**

The 11th Commandment
Wisdom from Our Children
by *The Children of America*

For all ages

"If there were an Eleventh Commandment, what would it be?" Children of many religious denominations across America answer this question—in their own drawings and words. "A rare book of spiritual celebration for all people, of all ages, for all time." —*Bookviews*
8 x 10, 48 pp, HC, Full-color illus., ISBN 1-879045-46-X **$16.95**

Children's Spirituality

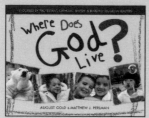

Where Does God Live?

by *August Gold*

Full-color illus. by *Matthew J. Perlman*

For ages
3–6

MULTICULTURAL, NONDENOMINATIONAL,
NONSECTARIAN

Using simple, everyday examples that children can relate to, this colorful book helps young readers develop a personal understanding of God.

10 x 8½, 32 pp, Quality PB, Full-color illus., ISBN 1-893361-39-X **$7.95**

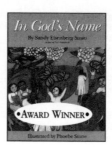

God's Paintbrush

For ages
4 & up

by *Sandy Eisenberg Sasso*; Full-color illus. by *Annette Compton*

Invites children of all faiths and backgrounds to encounter God openly in their own lives. Wonderfully interactive; provides questions adult and child can explore together at the end of each episode. "An excellent way to honor the imaginative breadth and depth of the spiritual life of the young." —Dr. Robert Coles, Harvard University

11 x 8½, 32 pp, HC, Full-color illus., ISBN 1-879045-22-2 **$16.95**

Also available: **A Teacher's Guide**

8½ x 11, 32 pp, PB, ISBN 1-879045-57-5 **$6.95**

God's Paintbrush Celebration Kit 9½ x 12, HC, Includes 5 sessions/40 full-color Activity Sheets and Teacher Folder with complete instructions, ISBN 1-58023-050-4 **$21.95**

In God's Name

For ages
4 & up

by *Sandy Eisenberg Sasso*; Full-color illus. by *Phoebe Stone*

Like an ancient myth in its poetic text and vibrant illustrations, this award-winning modern fable about the search for God's name celebrates the diversity and, at the same time, the unity of all the people of the world. "What a lovely, healing book!" —Madeleine L'Engle

9 x 12, 32 pp, HC, Full-color illus., ISBN 1-879045-26-5 **$16.95**

Children's Spirituality

God Said Amen

For ages 4 & up

by *Sandy Eisenberg Sasso*

Full-color illus. by *Avi Katz*

MULTICULTURAL, NONDENOMINATIONAL, NONSECTARIAN

A warm and inspiring tale of two kingdoms: Midnight Kingdom is overflowing with water but has no oil to light its lamps; Desert Kingdom is blessed with oil but has no water to grow its gardens. The kingdoms' rulers ask God for help but are too stubborn to ask each other. It takes a minstrel, a pair of royal riding-birds and their young keepers, and a simple act of kindness to show that they need only reach out to each other to find the answers to their prayers.

9 x 12, 32 pp, HC, Full-color illus., ISBN 1-58023-080-6 **$16.95**

For Heaven's Sake

For ages 4 & up

by *Sandy Eisenberg Sasso*; Full-color illus. by *Kathryn Kunz Finney*

Everyone talked about heaven: "Thank heavens." "Heaven forbid." "For heaven's sake, Isaiah." But no one would say what heaven was or how to find it. So Isaiah decides to find out, by seeking answers from many different people. "This book is a reminder of how well Sandy Sasso knows the minds of children. But it may surprise—and delight—readers to find how well she knows us grown-ups too." —Maria Harris, National Consultant in Religious Education, and author of *Teaching and Religious Imagination*
9 x 12, 32 pp, HC, Full-color illus., ISBN 1-58023-054-7 **$16.95**

But God Remembered

For ages 8 & up

Stories of Women from Creation to the Promised Land

by *Sandy Eisenberg Sasso*; Full-color illus. by *Bethanne Andersen*

A fascinating collection of four different stories of women only briefly mentioned in biblical tradition and religious texts. Award-winning author Sasso vibrantly brings to life courageous and strong women from ancient tradition; all teach important values through their actions and faith. "Exquisite. . . . A book of beauty, strength and spirituality." —Association of Bible Teachers 9 x 12, 32 pp, HC, Full-color illus., ISBN 1-879045-43-5 **$16.95**

God in Between

For ages 4 & up

by *Sandy Eisenberg Sasso*; Full-color illus. by *Sally Sweetland*

If you wanted to find God, where would you look? A magical, mythical tale that teaches that God can be found where we are: within all of us and the relationships between us. "This happy and wondrous book takes our children on a sweet and holy journey into God's presence." —Rabbi Wayne Dosick, Ph.D., author of *The Business Bible* and *Soul Judaism*
9 x 12, 32 pp, HC, Full-color illus., ISBN 1-879045-86-9 **$16.95**